The Little
iDVD
Book

Bob LeVitus

Peachpit Press • Berkeley, California

The Little iDVD Book

Bob LeVitus

Peachpit Press

1249 Eighth Street
Berkeley, CA 94710
510/524-2178
800/283-9444
510/524-2221 (fax)
Find us on the World Wide Web at: http://www.peachpit.com
Peachpit Press is a division of Pearson Education

Editor: Kate McKinley
Production Coordinators: Gloria Marquez, Kate Reber
Technical Editor: Victor Gavenda
Compositor: Owen Wolfson
Indexer: Karin Arrigoni
Cover Design: John Tollett and Mimi Heft
Cover Illustration: Bud Peen

ISBN 0-201-79533-7

9 8 7 6 5 4 3 2 1

For Allison and Jacob, who now understand the meaning of the word "deadline."

And for Lisa, who has always been the one.

For all three of you: I promise I'm going to try really hard to not work so hard anymore.

I love you all all the muches.

—BL
Summer 2002

Acknowledgements

First and foremost: Thank you for buying my book.

This book was a team effort. Though my name appears on the cover, it wouldn't exist without the extraordinary efforts of that team. And so, before we go any further, I'd like to take this opportunity to express my heartfelt gratitude to all of them...

Major thanks to Peachpit Press Publisher (try saying that three times fast) Nancy Ruenzel and Executive Editor Marjorie Baer, for believing in this project and giving it the green light.

Big time thanks to Kate Reber, production coordinator extraordinaire, for keeping the whole affair on track week in and week out, and to awesome freelance editor Kate McKinley, who not only minded my Ps and Qs, but managed to keep the word "stuff" from appearing on every page. I'd also like to thank Owen Wolfson, for composing these gorgeous pages in record time.

My super duper literary agent, Carole McClendon at Waterside Productions, deserves praise for stellar deal-making on my behalf, year in and year out.

And my wife, Lisa, and my kids, Allison and Jacob, have certainly earned very special thanks for putting up with my all-too-frequent hibernations, and giving me the space to do what I do. I love you guys all the muches.

I'm almost done...but I'd be remiss if I didn't also thank Apple—both for creating iDVD and pricing it right.

And last but certainly not least, very special thanks to Senior Technical Editor, Victor Gavenda, for excellent technical observations and insights too numerous to count (not to mention his extremely humorous editorial comments).

Table of Contents

Introduction

Way back in January 2001, Steve Jobs spoke about Apple leading the way into the "era of the digital lifestyle," and said that the Mac is the "digital hub" that allows you not only to enjoy digital content, but also to create it yourself in the comfort of your own home. At the time, I was somewhat skeptical; it sounded like yet another flavor of the infamous Cupertino Kool-Aid to me.

But hey, it's my sworn duty to check this stuff out for you, gentle reader. So, as I did before writing *The Little iTunes Book* (also from Peachpit), I've been doing a lot of research.

In the name of research, I've made movies and DVDs using iMovie 2 and iDVD 2, and their pro-quality brethren Final Cut Pro and DVD Studio Pro. (You'll hear more about both in Appendix A, "The Pit You Throw Money Into.") Anyway, today, with those igloo-lookin', flat-screen-swivelin', DVD burnin' iMacs going for less than $2,000, I'm happy to admit that I was way wrong and Steve was way right. The Mac has become the ultimate digital hub, just as he proclaimed it would.

Allow me to digress, just for a moment. In my previous life, before I became a full-time geek/raconteur (and before the phrase "desktop video" was even invented), I worked for an advertising agency in Los Angeles where one of my responsibilities was to produce television commercials. At that time, if you wanted to create video good enough to be shown on television, with transitions, synchronized sounds, multiple tracks, and special effects, you needed a pocket full of cash. Just *renting* a "broadcast-quality" video-editing suite could easily cost from $100 to more than $1,000 an hour.

Building an editing suite in those days would set you back hundreds of thousands of dollars. Today, I can do almost anything I could do in that million-dollar studio right here in my home office, for a fraction of the price. It used to cost me (actually, my client) $5,000 or $10,000 just to edit a single 30-second commercial; today, for less than $3,000 I can buy everything I need to make real broadcast-quality video—a SuperDrive-equipped Macintosh, Apple's iMovie 2 (or even Final Cut Pro), and an inexpensive digital video camcorder.

But, unlike those expensive post-production suites, I'm proud to say that my little studio also runs Microsoft Office, Quicken, Return to Castle Wolfenstein, and more than 15,000 other software titles, manages my email and Web site, and produces the manuscripts I sell, like this one you're reading. Oh, and it surfs the Web like the biggest Kahuna, burns audio and data CDs reliably and quickly, makes data and video DVDs, synchronizes with my iPod, and a whole bunch more. But the best part of all is that my studio is walking distance from my bedroom. Eat your heart out, Pacific Video!

The guts of my studio are a Power Macintosh G4 dual gigahertz tower with SuperDrive, two 17-inch computer monitors, a small NTSC monitor (in other words, a TV set with video-in), an extra gigabyte of RAM, Apple's iMovie, Final Cut Pro 2, iDVD, and DVD Studio Pro, a Canon ZR25 MC digital camcorder, and a bunch of other stuff. For around $8,000 I've built a video studio capable of producing honest-to-goodness broadcast-quality video even the major networks would be happy to transmit. And I can deliver it on a DVD to anyone with a recent-vintage set-top DVD player (or DVD-playing computer), for less than $5 a copy! What's not to love?

I've made a handful of short films and DVDs and I'm pretty darn proud of what I've accomplished so far.

I put the one I like best on my Apple Home Page at http://homepage.mac.com/boblevitus/ if you're interested.

I'm not saying that $8,000 worth of video-editing gear is going to turn you into a world-famous auteur. But it will give you the chance to try your hand at filmmaking without selling your soul or hocking your home.

And, in my humble opinion, the best part—without having to sell out to the Hollywood entertainment machine to tell your story visually.

Mark my words: Desktop video (DTV) is going to be the next big thing—bigger even than desktop publishing (DTP). And, like DTP, DTV is so much better on a Mac.

But you know that. You bought this book, didn't you?

The Dad Test

If you're one of the many who bought my 37th book, *The Little iTunes Book,* you surely remember the Dad test:

One day (pre-iTunes) when I was visiting my father, an avid but rather unsophisticated iMac user, I played one of my homemade CDs for him. He loved it. He then asked if I could show him how to make his own audio CDs. I thought back on all the trouble I'd had getting my setup working, the multistep process, the two separate programs he'd need, and the several system extensions he'd have to install. I also thought about the cost of buying the software and hardware. And I was forced to reply, "I'm afraid not."

Then I saw iTunes, a single, elegant program that manages your music collection effortlessly, rips songs from CD to hard disk quickly and easily, burns custom audio CDs painlessly (and without taking over your entire Mac), and displays some of the coolest visual effects I've ever seen. It was the first MP3 program that could pass my "Dad test" with flying colors: I could teach Dad enough about it in half an hour to have him burning custom CDs to his heart's content.

Sadly, Dad's not around to test iDVD. He'd have loved it and it would have passed the Dad test easily. But...

I do have this neighbor with a Dell PC. When "Dave" (not his real name) saw my first iMovies more than a year ago, he asked if he could do that on his Dell, running some variation of Windows. Like any good doctor, my first response was, "Don't do dat!"

I tried to explain that while he probably could, he'd need some additional hardware and software, and that even then it probably wouldn't work as well as an inexpensive Mac. I told him that every single Mac includes everything you need to edit video—computer, proper video card and drivers, FireWire ports, big fast hard drive. "Just add camcorder." He didn't want to abandon his beloved Dull (er—Dell), so he bought a new one, with all the hardware and software they told him he needed to edit video "just like on a Mac." Later, I showed him some of the work I'd done in preparing to write this book, then I asked how his video editing was going. He replied that he hadn't quite gotten it working yet and still hadn't made a single movie. Meanwhile, I'd made dozens of videos and DVDs.

Then, the new iMac came out, and the rest is history. With DVD-burning now available on a killer computer priced below $2,000.... Well, you know the rest.

Excerpt from "I'm sorry, Dave. I'm afraid you can't do that (at least not on a Dell...)"

I lent him the new iMac for a few days and issued a challenge. Since he still, 18 months later, had not completed a single movie project on his Dell, I told him to try making a movie, an audio CD, and a DVD on this iMac. And to make things interesting, I offered him no assistance or support—I told him to look in Mac Help if he had questions.

Three days later I interviewed "Dave."

On the first day, he unpacked the iMac, set it up in 5 minutes, and burned two audio CDs with iTunes. He said he never needed to refer to Mac Help and that this whole project was "no problem whatsoever."

On the second day, he used iDVD to create a pair of slide shows using existing digital photos and burned his first DVD. I watched it later and it didn't stink. In fact, most people would no doubt find it impressive. (I'm so jaded...)

On the third day, he borrowed my Canon ZR-25 camcorder and a tape of my son's last basketball game. I handed him the camera, manual, and FireWire cable and told him, "You're on your own." By the end of the day he had imported raw footage into iMovie, edited it, added music and titles, then burned it onto a DVD with iDVD.

As I scribbled furiously, Dave's long-suffering wife added, "He swore less at the Mac than he does at his Dell."

Dave then said he had created more multimedia in three days with the iMac than he had in 18 months with his Dell. He only opened the Help file a couple of times. He concluded, "the hardest part was getting the iMac back in the box."

Before departing, I asked if he'd consider a Mac next time. He replied, "Absolutely. In fact, if we hadn't wasted so much money trying to transform that Dell into a multimedia computer, I'd get one today."

It was music to my ears.

Copyright ©2002 Bob LeVitus. Used by permission.

This piece originally appeared in my "Dr. Mac" column in the *Houston Chronicle* on March 29, 2002. My point was this: The desktop video revolution is here and Apple is clearly leading the way. iMovie 2 and Final Cut Pro make it easy and affordable to make movies with your Mac; iDVD 2 and DVD Studio Pro make it easy and (more or less) affordable to create high-quality DVDs.

And it's all so easy, even a kid can do it. If that's not a revolution, I don't know what is.

Who Should Read This Book

Everyone should read this book, of course, even people who use Windows computers. (My accountant made me say that—iDVD is, of course, a Mac-only program.)

All kidding aside, this book is for anyone and everyone who uses iDVD. More specifically, it's for people who want to know more about the program and about making DVDs than they'll find in the iDVD Help system. But most of all, it's for iDVD users who want to learn how to burn better DVDs.

Since iDVD is still a relatively new application, I make very few assumptions in this book, but I do assume that you know the basics of using your Mac, such as how to turn it on, launch a program, insert a disc, click, double-click, use menus, create folders, and so on.

If you're fuzzy on any of those concepts, I recommend you read one of Robin Williams's Peachpit books for beginners— The Little Mac Book, The Little iMac Book, The Little iBook Book, or The Little Mac OS X Book (which is not in any way little)—before you dig into this one.

How to Use This Book

The world of digital video uses specialized terms such as *MPEG* and *bit rate* and also uses some ordinary words such as *burn* and *rip* in special ways. Rather then stick the definitions in a Glossary at the end of the book where you'll never see it, I've tried to define each term when I first use it. If you forget a term, you can always check the Index to find that definition. I also use several icons to highlight parts of the text.

The Note icon tells you that the accompanying text is not essential, though if I bothered to include it and my editors didn't bother to cut it, it's probably interesting or even useful.

The Tip icon tells you that the accompanying text contains an important time-saving tip or trick that it would be helpful to learn.

The Warning icon is only used when what I'm saying is so important that ignoring it could have disastrous consequences. I don't use warning icons often in this book, so if you see one, read carefully.

All righty, then—let's move along to the fun stuff.

P.S. While I can't promise to answer every email message I receive, I do try to answer as many as I can. If you have a comment about this book, or a question about something I've written in it, please feel free to send me a message; I'll try my best to answer in a timely fashion. My email address is lidvd@boblevitus.com.

part 1

Basic Training

In the Beginning

When I was just a pup there was no such thing as a DVD. Heck, back then the "VHS vs. Beta wars" hadn't even been fought yet, much less won by the technically inferior format backed by a coalition of slightly-less-greedy-than-Sony hardware manufacturers. Instant photography meant a Polaroid camera, expensive film, and a smelly goop stick for "fixing" the pictures. And the audiocassette was considered the biggest breakthrough in music technology since the 8-track tape.

Today DVD is poised to surpass the compact disc as the dominant medium of exchange for digital data. Most Macs (and many other computers) can now read DVDs, and computers equipped with a DVD-R drive (like the Apple SuperDrive) can burn video or more than 4 GB of data on blank discs that cost less than $5 each. Best of all, the video DVDs you create can be viewed on most set-top DVD players, which are becoming common in American homes, and the data discs can be read by any Mac (or PC) with a DVD player.

We've come a long way, baby.

In this, our first chapter together, we'll start out nice and easy with a bit of background on the technologies that make the whole thing—video, audio, editing, and disc-burning—work: QuickTime, FireWire, and SuperDrive (and, of course, a Macintosh). Then we'll have a brief overview, from beginning to end, of the process of making a DVD, so you have some idea of what it takes to produce a disc. Finally, we'll take a quick peek at the object of our newfound affection, iDVD itself.

A (Tiny) Bit of Background

I won't spend much time on this, but before you embark on this journey—making your own video DVDs containing high-quality digital video, animated menus, and more—I feel you should have some idea of how things were in the old days. I think it'll help you understand why burning your own DVDs is so cool.

The Mac has been the tool of creative thinkers since its introduction in 1984. In fact, one of the first and most popular non-business, non-game Mac programs in those early days was a brilliant little program called VideoWorks from an eccentric little company called MacroMind.

 VideoWorks grew into Director, MacroMind grew into the publicly held Macromedia, and VideoWorks co-creator Marc Canter grew louder and richer.

Of course, in spite of its name, VideoWorks wasn't "real" video— it was more like "CartoonWorks." And though it was fun, and neat, it couldn't make the same stuff as you saw on TV.

Back then, when SEs and Pluses ruled the Earth, Macs were pretty much incapable of working with video. They lacked expansion, hard disk capacity, RAM, internal bus bandwidth (a *bus* is a pathway for data inside your computer), and any type of high-speed data bus, to mention a few.

NuBus slots and SCSI ports, introduced in the early '90s, were a step in the right direction, but Macs (and indeed, most personal computers) still lacked sufficient horsepower to process video efficiently or effectively.

Does anyone remember VideoSpigot? It was the first cheap ($200) NuBus video capture card. In the early days of QuickTime, everyone I knew bought one and made lots of great little postage-stamp-size movies (using Premiere 1.0, no less).

The point is that until recently, video production and post-production were still the exclusive domain of the million-dollar editing suites I mentioned in the introduction, and far out of the reach of the common computer user.

The Titanic Triumvirate

Then, a trio of cutting-edge technologies reached critical mass and maturity simultaneously. The result of that convergence, as they say, is history.

Yes, friends, I'm going on the record as saying that this whole "edit professional-quality video for under three grand" idea exists almost exclusively because of three all-important technologies (two of them invented by Apple Computer and the third merely popularized by Apple).

QuickTime, FireWire, and SuperDrive are these three technological marvels. The combination of the three, mixed as only Apple could mix them, is the special sauce that lets us create pro-quality (more or less) DVDs on inexpensive iMacs.

And without them? Let's just say you might not be making DVDs; I wouldn't be writing this book; iMovie, iDVD, iPhoto, and iTunes might not exist (they rely on QuickTime or FireWire or both); and Apple might not be in business today. That's how important I believe these three technologies are to Apple and to "video for the masses."

Here's how these parts fit together.

QuickTime

Reduced to the lowest common denominator, QuickTime is a file format. More technically (or at least according to that revered arbiter of the technical, the Apple Web site), Quick-Time is software that allows Mac (and Windows) users to play back audio and video on their computers. But taking a deeper look, QuickTime is many things: a file format, an environment for media authoring, and a suite of applications that includes QuickTime Player, QuickTime Pro, the QuickTime browser plug-in, and more.

Just recently, Apple announced the next version of QuickTime—version 6. But I'm pretty sure it won't be out until after the release of this book. So when I say "QuickTime," assume the version I'm talking about is version 5 even if you're using version 6.

So QuickTime isn't just a format or single program, it's a suite of programs, underlying technologies, architectures, and file format(s).

QuickTime's function is a bit easier to define. It's the part of the Mac OS that lets you create, save, manage, manipulate, and deliver rich-media documents. As a format, it's extremely flexible. QuickTime documents can include any combination of video, audio, interactivity, text, HTML, logic, and still pictures, to name just a few.

QuickTime has been under constant development at Apple for more than 10 years and has become a standard in both video and interactive media authoring and production. And its extensible architecture ensures that QuickTime will still be around 10 years from now—it's designed to accommodate future media types and file formats, even ones that haven't been invented yet.

FireWire

If QuickTime is the production facility for authoring rich media, FireWire is the truck that brings raw materials in and takes finished goods out.

FireWire is sometimes called IEEE 1394 or i.Link (mostly by vendors too cheap to pay Apple for use of the official FireWire trademark). Many FireWire peripherals (mostly scanners and storage devices, including the iPod) don't need AC power as long as they are connected to a Mac by FireWire. One distinguishing characteristic of i.Link is that it uses a four-pin connector, rather than the six-pin connector on your Mac. The missing two pins carry power to the device, so i.Link devices (mostly camcorders) can't take their power off the FireWire bus.

FireWire is a registered trademark of Apple Computer.

In simple terms, FireWire is a cable that lets you connect to your Macintosh things that need a fast connection—like DV camcorders, scanners, hard disks, and DVD burners.

More technically (again, according to Apple), FireWire is "a high-speed serial input/output technology for connecting digital devices such as digital camcorders and cameras to desktop and portable computers."

FireWire is blazing fast and mostly trouble-free.

Before FireWire, the Mac high-speed interface standard was SCSI (short for "small computer systems interface"; pronounced "skuzzy"), an exceptionally temperamental bus that became exponentially more cranky as you added more SCSI devices. And each device had to be assigned a special SCSI ID number and there were all kinds of SCSI conflicts and…

Just trust me on this: FireWire is a walk in the park compared to SCSI.

After SCSI came USB (short for "universal serial bus"), which was slow (fast enough for keyboards, mice, speakers, and such, but slow if used for storage) and much better-tempered, but not without its quirks. Soon after, FireWire arrived, and it moves data at up to 400 megabits per second (Mbps), up to 30 times faster than USB. Furthermore, unlike SCSI devices, most FireWire devices can be "hot swapped." That means you don't have to shut down or restart to add or remove most FireWire devices. Just plug them in and they work. It's like magic. And you can connect up to 63 of them at a time on a single FireWire bus!

> *USB devices are supposed to be hot-swappable too, but USB hot-swapping doesn't always work.*

All of this taken together is probably why FireWire has become the interface of choice for today's digital audio and video devices, as well as for external hard drives and other high-speed peripherals.

> *Not all FireWire devices are happy with hot-swapping. Since there's no way for me to know what kind of device you have, all I'm going to tell you is to read the manual for your device to learn the correct procedure for connecting and disconnecting it.*

FireWire is standard on every single Mac built today and is also built into almost every single digital video camera ever made. In just a few short years it's become the de facto standard for the video industry and is a big part of the reason Macintosh remains the platform of choice for anyone creating rich media, audio, or video.

To find out more about QuickTime and FireWire—and there's lots more to find out—visit www.apple.com/quicktime and www.apple.com/firewire, respectively.

DVD-R

Last but not least, we mustn't overlook the contribution of DVD technology (it stands for "digital versatile disc" or "digital video disc," depending upon whom you ask). With inexpensive set-top DVD players sold on every corner, Apple driving the price of blank DVD-R discs down below the $5 mark, and many computers offering at least DVD playback, if not both playback and recording, it's no wonder that DVD is becoming the standard for digital media as well as for data storage and backup.

But in addition to being a big, fat, cheap storage medium, there's this: DVD is the first consumer medium to offer interactivity that *isn't* tied to a computer or a Web connection. With DVD, your interactive work, with its menus and buttons, can be played by anyone, using almost any cheap DVD player and TV.

So there you have it—QuickTime, FireWire, and SuperDrive DVD-R—the titanic triumverate. Now let's look at the actual process of making a DVD.

How to Make a DVD: The Short Version

Since this whole book is, more or less, about how to make a DVD, for now I'll give you the overview from 35,000 feet of the DVD-making process from start to finish.

When I first got iDVD and a SuperDrive, I took this free Apple online seminar called *DVD Authoring Made Easy*. It was great— I had worked with video a lot in the past but didn't have much experience with interactivity. I thought Apple's five-step process made sense and I've followed it for almost every DVD project I've undertaken since.

If the seminar is still available you'll find it at http://seminars.apple.com/seminarsonline.

Those five steps are Plan, Create, Encode, Author, and Record. Let's take a brief look at each.

Step 1: Plan

Well duh. Of course the first step is to plan. But since very few of us have ever actually made a DVD, what are some of the things that need planning?

Here's a partial list to get you started:

- **Who is the viewer?** Develop appropriate material for the target audience.

- **What is the project's purpose?** What are you trying to accomplish? Sell something? Entertain? Evoke emotions? Nailing it now will benefit you later.

- **What video, audio, still graphic, and other assets need to be created or assembled?** Some of this will have to wait until after Step 2, but it's a good idea to start this list early and consult it often. You don't want to get to the end of a project and discover you forgot to cover a key shot.

- **Budget** Now is the time to determine out-of-pocket costs (if any). Then triple them.

- **End date** The final due date or deadline. All other milestones are figured out backward from here.

- **Milestones** Milestones I use include storyboard and script approval, all assets in-house, all editing completed, rough cut (of DVD), and end date.

Keep in mind that this is the list for making a DVD. There is (or at least there should be) a similar list for actually shooting your video, which is a whole nother subject and one you could write a book on. And, in fact, Michael Rubin has done just that. If you want to know more about the video-making process, check out his Little Digital Video Book, *also from Peachpit.*

You should probably storyboard the DVD itself, as well as each individual video segment (this is highly recommended; see Chapter 2). And now is a good time to start developing the script, as well.

Many people skip the planning phase or gloss over it. That's a bad idea. Planning may be the most important part of the process. I can promise you that the time you spend planning will be repaid to you in abundance when you finish your project on time and without having to redo much (if any) of it.

Step 2: Create

This is the part where you make or find all the different media pieces that will eventually be part of your DVD. In this phase you'll

- Write a script
- Shoot and edit video
- Create art
- Create titles
- Create the soundtrack
- Create navigational elements

This step tends to be the most time-consuming, so after you determine how many hours you think all your content creation is going to take, double or triple it.

Step 3: Encode

Before you can make a DVD, you need to convert all of the elements into a format DVD players understand—MPEG 2 for video and AIFF or AC3 for audio. The good news is that with iDVD and QuickTime on your team, you don't have to do much. Just create your DVD project using QuickTime-compatible files (that includes a lot of different file formats, by the way). Then work with those files until your masterpiece is complete. When you click Burn DVD, iDVD handles all of the encoding to MPEG 2, AIFF, or AC3 for every element in your project, all behind the scenes and without your having to lift a finger.

The downside is that you don't have control over data rates or image quality in iDVD. Its defaults will probably be fine for 95 percent of what you want to do. If you need more horsepower, Apple's professional DVD authoring tool, DVD Studio Pro, lets you encode video at any data rate and author media for a wide variety of DVD formats. It's discussed in Appendix A.

Step 4: Author

In hip multimedia parlance, *authoring* means the creative melding of video, audio, and graphics into an interactive DVD with menus, buttons, soundtrack(s), and subtitles or alternative language.

This is where iDVD comes in. It's a DVD-grinder (well, officially, it's known as a *DVD authoring program*). Just pour in your raw ingredients—video, sound, pictures, menus, buttons, and so on—add a little elbow grease, and out pops a fully formed video DVD with all the bells and whistles, that can be played on almost any cheap DVD player.

If you were conscientious about Steps 1 and 2, Step 4 will be painless and fun. If you weren't, it won't.

Indeed, iDVD is the easiest, fastest, most intuitive program you can use to author a DVD. But you knew that.

Step 5: Burn

Preview and adjust your magnum opus in iDVD, and when you're happy with everything about it, there's just one thing left to do—click the Burn button. And iDVD does the rest.

I know it sounds simple, but this may be the scariest step of all. If you make a mistake in any of the other steps, as long as you catch it before you burn, it won't cost you a penny. But make a mistake here and you're out $5 (but you will have a shiny new $5 coaster you can use to protect your furniture from unsightly stains and rings).

A Short Pictorial

Since the parts of this book that aren't about how to make a DVD are about how to use iDVD, in this section I'll give you an overview of what iDVD looks like and what some of its parts do. This time I'll do it using pictures, which I hope are worth several thousand words each.

Figure 1.1 is a big picture of the Big Picture.

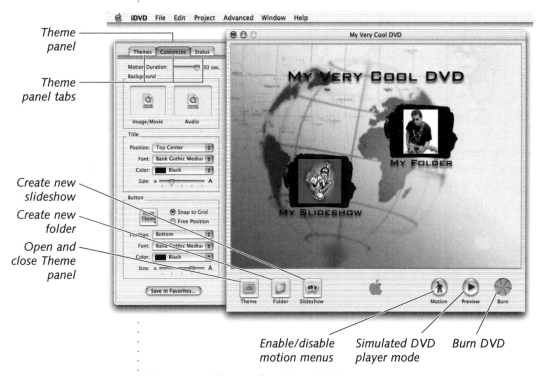

Figure 1.1 This, my friends, is iDVD.

One of the first things you'll do when you begin working with iDVD is import video and other elements into your project. This being a Macintosh and all, while there is an Import item in the File menu, it's even easier to just drag your media files onto iDVD, as shown in **Figure 1.2.**

One of iDVD's greatest strengths is the ease of changing the look and feel of your DVD project by selecting a different theme in the Theme panel, as shown in **Figure 1.3.**

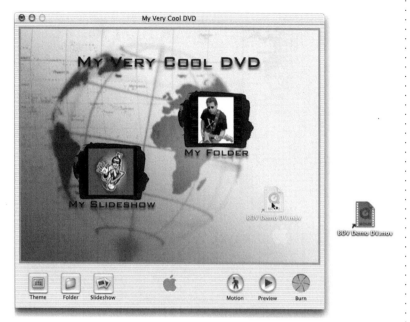

Figure 1.2 Getting movies into iDVD is as easy as dragging and dropping.

Figure 1.3 The joy of themes—one click gets you a whole new look.

Another simple pleasure is that iDVD lets you make a slideshow out of digital still photos, as shown in **Figure 1.4.**

Figure 1.4
Making a slideshow part of your DVD is a cinch.

Before you commit to burning a $5 disc, use iDVD's preview mode (complete with a cute little remote control) to check your work, as shown in **Figure 1.5.**

OK. That'll be about enough of that. We're going to get back to this fun stuff shortly, but first there are things you need to know before you even think about burning a DVD. Which happens to be the title of Chapter 2.

Figure 1.5
Clever how they simulate a remote control on the screen, don't you think?

Before You Even Think About Burning a DVD

Before you burn a single disc—heck, before you even launch iMovie or iDVD again, read this chapter. It is my attempt to cover every single thing, small and large, you'll want to consider before you start any DVD project.

Don't get me wrong. I know that every DVD project is different and that some will require extensive planning and pre-production while others turn out fantastic, even though created "on the fly" with little or no forethought.

Whether your project is big, small, or in-between, when you set out to create a DVD from scratch, there's a lot to consider—and perhaps reject—before you shoot an inch of footage, spend a single penny, or expend one ounce of additional effort on it.

I'm not going to tell you that you have to do every single thing this chapter suggests before every single project. But I am going to suggest that you need to at least *know* about all the things in this chapter. You see, I firmly believe that when you plan a project, if you choose to ignore any of this, it should be because you choose to ignore it, not because you forgot or didn't know.

Much of this chapter will be expanded upon here and there in upcoming parts of the book. And for your convenience, I've included a handy preproduction checklist at the end of this chapter.

Planning to Start Planning

In Chapter 1, I said that planning may be the most important part of the whole process. You'll hear me say that a lot. But I also understand the human need to just roll up your sleeves and do it.

So, even if you choose to devote only a few minutes to planning your DVD project, this chapter will help you use those few minutes wisely.

I've found that the time I spend planning a project is almost always repaid with interest when I finish on time (or early), on budget (or under), and without having a lot of "do-overs" (if any) because of poor planning.

You may notice that much of this book isn't actually about *iDVD itself. That's entirely by design. Frankly, iDVD is so easy to use that even if I were at my most verbose, if all I did was explain how to use iDVD, this book would have to be titled* The Extremely Short iDVD Book. *So though the title is* The Little iDVD Book, *it's actually about how to make good DVDs with iDVD, which requires a lot more than just a copy of iDVD and a SuperDrive.*

One last thing: I'm going to cover these items in the order I consider them when I'm working on my own projects. Your style may be different, so feel free to combine steps, change the order of them, or even omit them. It's your project; this chapter is just food for thought before you fall too much in love with your project to think clearly.

Make Some Notes

I'm an inveterate note-taker. I always have a pad and pen in my pocket and another in my car. Once I decide to do a project (or even consider doing a project), I create a new folder on my hard disk for it. That way everything, or at least all the digital elements—all my notes, materials, files, movies, pictures, scripts, and so on—will be in one place throughout the production. Some projects also require a physical container, like a file folder or envelope, for non-digital documents, paperwork, and other stuff I can't store on my hard drive.

I know the checklist at the end of the chapter like the back of my hand. Whenever I think about any element of any project, I jot it down immediately. If I'm at my Mac, I type it into my project overview document. If I'm away from the computer, I write a note and stuff it in my pocket. When I get back to my office, I empty my pocket onto the desk and transfer my notes from paper into my project overview document.

Make an outline

I almost always start by creating an outline for the project. I like outlines. I've been using an outliner on my Mac since Think-Tank 512 for Mac in the late '80s. Almost every project I do—writing, video, DVD, presentation, whatever—starts as an outline.

Outlining lets me easily hide and show levels of detail in my document, move chunks around quickly, easily, and visually with drag and drop, and organize the order and grouping of elements and sub-elements painlessly. The outline metaphor works for me when planning and managing projects and it always has.

Microsoft Word has an outline mode, and that's what I use to plan most writing projects. It's not the most intuitive outliner I've used, but once you get the hang of it, it's quite powerful. Since I use Word all the time anyway, I use the Word outliner a lot. (See **Figure 2.1.**)

If you're not a Word user, another nice outlining solution is the inexpensive ($21.12 per seat) OmniOutliner, a gorgeous and easy-to-use outliner. OmniOutliner was developed exclusively for Mac OS X in native Cocoa, so it takes full advantage of everything OS X has to offer and is Aqua-licious as well. It's well suited to the type of project outlines you might create for a DVD. (See **Figure 2.2.**)

> *You can download a free demo of OmniOutliner at www.omnigroup.com/applications/omnioutliner.*

Figure 2.1
I used Microsoft Word v.X's outliner for the master outline of this book.

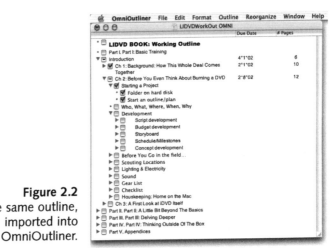

Figure 2.2
The same outline, imported into OmniOutliner.

Before I leave the subject of outlines and outliners, some people are more comfortable with a visual approach instead of outlining. If you're not hip to outlining, there's another Omni program, OmniGraffle, that you might prefer. It's another Cocoa/Aqua-licious offering for creating diagrams, family trees, flow charts, organization charts, layouts, and graphs, as shown in **Figure 2.3.** You can download a free demo version of this $59.95 program at www.omnigroup.com/applications/omnigraffle.

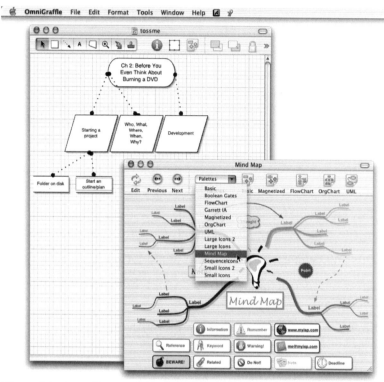

Figure 2.3 A small part of the same outline, imported into OmniGraffle.

The bigger the project, the more helpful and timesaving a good planning and tracking system will be. And I've always found that you'll save time and effort later if you organize all the disparate parts of your project in one place sooner.

It really doesn't matter if you use Word, OmniOutliner, OmniGraffle, Stickies, the Finder, or even your memory if it's good enough, to keep track of the elements that make up this project. What's important is that you keep track of them somehow.

Define your objectives

I try to start every project—regardless of its nature—by asking myself the Five W Questions, before I invest any more time in it:

1. **Who** is the audience? Who am I making this project for?

2. **What** is the purpose of this project?

3. **Where** are the production facilities and locations I'll use in this project?

4. **When** does it have to be completed?

5. **Why** am I doing it?

I admit it's a journalism technique, but it only takes a few minutes and it can really help you define the project more clearly. A lot of later decisions will be based on the answers to these five Ws, so I usually put this at the top of any project checklist and work through it first.

Next, I create a "one-sentence pitch" for my project. I try to describe what I want to do in a single sentence. This helps tighten my focus even further.

"This DVD will be sent to Mom, Dad, and Aunt Shana so they can see how big the kids have grown since last summer."

"This DVD will contain a product demo for potential investors."

"This is an instructional DVD to be sold through direct-response advertising."

"This is a music video to promote my band's new recording project."

And so on.

Road Mapping (a.k.a. Development)

I think of the development phase as assembling all the road maps you need before you begin production—script, storyboards, shot lists, and so on. (The actual production process—shooting and editing, for the most part—will be covered in Chapter 4.)

Much of what I think of as the development process depends on the purpose of the disc you're making. A project for family and friends requires one kind of road map: I would map out something polished enough to impress them while only taking a few hours of my time to complete.

If the project is for the soccer team I coach, it's a completely different road map. For them I would do nothing fancy: No editing, no titles, not much time spent; just what they need, which is footage of plays worth watching.

> *This worked great. We shot the entire game as one continuous wide shot. I reviewed the footage, culled out the best plays, and burned the whole thing, unedited, onto a DVD. I had the team over for pizza and plays one night. When we watched it on my cheap Korean DVD player and expensive Japanese big-screen TV, the video was as clear as a photograph and the freeze-frame images, when we stopped the action to discuss a play or player's position, were almost as clear. Everyone loved it: the team (kids love seeing themselves on TV), the parents (who think I'm a cross between Steven Spielberg and Pelé), and me, too. If you have a kid in sports or know one, give it a try. It's a blast.*

If it's for a client or for a business pitch, it's another road map entirely. I know I need to end up with a product that is polished, professional, and offers good production values. This road map would be a full-blown production in itself—script, budget, daily breakdowns, screenings for the client, and so on.

Finally, discs I do just for me are another case entirely—their maps can cover almost anything, including all of the above.

> *But they're often parodies. I can't help myself. I like making fake commercials and music videos. To me, that's fun. Your mileage may vary.*

So let's say, just for giggles, that you have a crystal-clear conception of your audience, purpose, places, times, and reason. Now it's time to dig in and "develop" the project.

Script

Most projects require a script. Put another way, if anybody on-screen is supposed to say anything, somebody has to write those words for them. And if there's narration, someone has to write that, too.

In a looser sense of the word, just about anything you intend to capture on video ought to be "scripted." Which is why, in some cases, you won't bother with a script and will make do with just a shot list.

Shot list

If you're planning to use video and not planning to use a script, at least make a shot list. It's just what it sounds like: a list of *all* the shots you need to complete your video (and, by extension, your DVD).

I call shooting this way "documentary-style," and it often results in great video. But I find it works more consistently if I give some thought to the shots I need to tell the story, before I pick up the camera. I try to always plan the shots I'm going to need before I head off to shoot something. Even a short list helps. At worst, make a list in your head at the last minute.

For example, my daughter and a friend were washing my car in the driveway one day. They looked really cute doing it, so I asked them if they wanted to be in a car wash movie. Of course they were thrilled. I very quickly cranked out a shot list, set up a boom-box playing some funky dance music, turned on the camera, and said to the girls, "Dance, sing, be outrageous, and have fun."

Here's the shot list I wrote in the 2 minutes between deciding to make this video and picking up the camera:

- Master coverage of car washing: Wide to ECU (extreme close-up)
- Footage of girls dancing by car with towels
- Close-up of side mirror with reflections of girls dancing with towels
- Close-up of hands washing license plate, side mirror, wheels
- Shots of soap bucket
- Shots of shiny car parts
- Whatever…

I shot about 10 minutes of raw footage and ended up with a very cute 3-minute ersatz MTV video of the girls, which everyone said was "adorable."

The more complex (and longer) your project, the more important it is to think about what video coverage you're going to need and what scripting needs to be done before you shoot.

Storyboard

A storyboard is a sequence of drawings that represent what you're supposed to see on-screen. Think of the storyboard (and script and shot list) as the road map of what the viewer will see and hear.

For a television commercial or feature film there might be dozens or hundreds of professional drawings showing point-of-view, camera angle, and composition for all (or most) of the shots in the work. For a casual video/DVD maker, it might just be brief text descriptions of each shot.

Storyboarding is separate from the script and the shot list for a reason. Regardless of what you choose to do with either of those, you need at least two storyboards for a DVD project— one for (each) video sequence and another for the DVD menus and control interface.

Here's a quick and dirty interface storyboard I whipped up for one of my famous family DVDs:

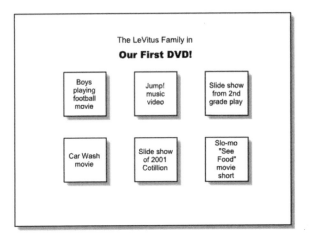

And here's how it turned out:

If a video sequence is going to have more than a few scenes in it, you need to think about what will be on the screen at any given moment. The storyboard, shot list, and script can help you figure that out before it's too late. And if your interface is going to go beyond Apple's template (or even if it's not), you need a storyboard for your menus and interface.

Schedule

A schedule is another road map worth developing, particularly if you have much time or money riding on the project. The bigger the project, the more important it is to create a workable schedule before you start. How many days will it take to write a script, storyboard, and shot list? How many days of shooting? How many hours or days of editing? How much time to finish the project in iDVD?

For your first few DVDs, everything is going to take twice as long as you expect. Don't let it get you down. As you become more familiar with the process, you'll get faster at it, and better, too.

Budget

Finally, if you need to buy or rent equipment, rent locations, hire personnel, contract talent, clear music rights, or spend any out-of-pocket cash on a project, you should create a budget.

Even if this DVD is only for yourself, little things have a way of costing you during production—extra sets of batteries, the cable you had to have express delivered, the discs you burned before you should have and had to throw away, and so on. If you're concerned, itemize the costs before you "green-light" the project.

Just make the darned road maps

You can do your road mapping the old-fashioned way with pen(cil) and paper, or use any of the myriad programs for Mac OS X such as FinalDraft for scripts (www.finaldraft.com); Adobe Photoshop, Photoshop Elements, or GraphicConverter for graphics (www.adobe.com and www.graphicconverter.net); OmniGraffle for diagramming and storyboarding (www.omnigroup.com); and Microsoft Office v.X for outlines, scripts, presentations, spreadsheets, storyboards, contact database, and calendar.

The whole point is: Every project needs a road map. If you start without one, you're likely to become lost.

If you have a good set of road maps before you set out, you know where you're going and why you're going there, as well as the result you desire. I promise that if you plan your journey well, you won't waste *too* much time getting there.

Further Considerations

But that isn't all there is to planning. No, not by a long shot. There is still much to consider before you roll an inch of tape or put laser to disc. A lot of this section relates to one part of the roadmap or another, and all of it—location, lighting, 'lectricity, and sound—requires at least a passing thought as you plan your project.

Locations

If you have to shoot "on location," you want to maintain as much control over the environment as you possibly can. If you have a choice between shooting a conversation in a crowded restaurant or at your own kitchen table, you're far better off in your kitchen, where you can control external elements such as sound and lights.

If you must shoot in an "uncontrolled" environment, scout the location in advance and see what the challenges are. Some locations require specialized gear—a taller tripod, a shotgun mic, a sun gun, or whatever—and you won't have what you need on hand if you don't scout.

Whenever possible, bring your camcorder and microphone on scouting missions and shoot as much test footage as you can. Check the tape carefully on an NTSC monitor, television, or Mac and the best speakers you have, for any signs of video interference or audio hum or buzz.

Lighting

If you plan on shooting in a low-light situation, particularly outdoors, you're going to need a light or lights. We'll talk more about how important lighting is to the quality of your digital video in Chapter 4. For now, just remember that the better the lighting, the better your footage will look.

If you can, bring a small television set or a PowerBook (and all the cables you'll need to connect them to your camcorder) to your shoots. Use that to review your footage. Check the lighting, details, and colors carefully; a TV or PowerBook can display what you're going to see on the final DVD far more accurately than the little 3-inch display on your camcorder.

Electricity

Are you going to need electrical power? If you end up having to rent lighting gear, how much of it will you be able to hook up without blowing a circuit? If you're considering lights, consider your electrical needs, too.

Sound

Location sound recording is extremely hard to do well with the built-in microphone in most camcorders. They're just not very good at recording dialog, though they can be used effectively for capturing monolog and ambient sounds under ideal situations.

> *Consider buying or renting a lavaliere microphone or two, or a boom or shotgun microphone if you want to record quality audio in the field.*

Beware of street noise, plumbing sounds, birds tweeting outside the window, heating and cooling vents, and things like that. They may not sound loud while you're shooting, but they're often quite audible when you play back your video.

> *Sometimes you can get away with muzzling a noisy pipe or vent with pillows, carpet, or other sound-deadening material. And sometimes you can just time your shots between their noises. But be aware of the audio environment if you hope to use audio from the field.*

Remember what I said about lighting a few paragraphs ago? About bringing a television to the shoot for reference? You should also bring a good set of headphones (familiarly known as *cans*) so you can monitor the audio for noise during recording and playback.

> *If a location is extremely inhospitable to sound recording, consider shooting the scene MOS. That's short for "mit out sound." It's an old film-school expression said to have originated with some old director who had a thick accent and couldn't pronounce the word* with.

If you have to shoot MOS, think about whether you can cover with music, narration, voiceover, or titles instead of live audio. MOS is often the only way to shoot a scene when using live audio would be impossible.

Housekeeping: Back Home on the Mac

The last piece of the preproduction puzzle we'll examine before playing with iDVD in Chapter 3 is checking out your Mac to make sure it's up to the task before you get started. Not just any Mac is ready to perform feats like authoring multimedia.

Here are some things to consider.

Disk space

You need a massive quantity of disk space available when you work with digital video. DV requires around 3.6 MB of storage space per second. So each minute of DV footage uses 220 MB, 10 minutes uses 2.2 GB, and 100 minutes uses more than 22 GB. But when you take into account all the interim versions, render files, and unused footage, you need three or four times as much storage as the final edited and encoded project will use.

If you don't have enough storage for the project, it's better to add more now than to bring the project to a crashing halt because there's no more disk space available.

I didn't have enough available storage space to write a book on DV and DVDs. So I ordered two 60 GB FireWire drives (7,200 RPM, with the speedy Oxford 911 FireWire bridge chipset). They cost $229.99 each from Other World Computing (www.macsales.com) and look like this:

Now I have plenty of room for any DV projects, and I shoot all the video I want, knowing I have plenty of disk space back home on the Mac. It's a nice feeling.

The rest of your Mac

The official system requirements for iDVD are a Power Mac G4 running Mac OS X version 10.1 or later, with an Apple SuperDrive and a minimum of 256 MB of RAM installed, with 384 MB recommended.

If your G4 Mac didn't come with a SuperDrive, you aren't completely out of luck. Pioneer (Apple's SuperDrive supplier) sells a SuperDrive equivalent. However, the drive—the Pioneer DVR-A03—must be installed internally in a G4 to work. External drives will not work with iDVD.

I recommend at least 512 MB of RAM for multimedia authoring, especially if you want to use iMovie or another video editing program and iDVD at the same time. It can be done and works beautifully, but not on a Mac with a mere 256 MB of RAM. Mac OS X loves RAM—if you don't have enough, performance will suffer. While virtual memory in OS X is an order of magnitude better than in OS 9, it's still not desirable when you're in a hurry. More RAM equals more performance. And who doesn't like that?

If you haven't used them lately, or haven't used them at all, it wouldn't hurt to make sure the software tools you need— iDVD and iMovie, at the very least—are installed and working properly. Save a finished movie or two in iMovie for use with iDVD. Burn a disc or two to make sure they work (be sure to review them on your set-top DVD player, and not just on your Mac).

Backup plan

All this digital video that uses up 220 MB of disk space per minute is valuable stuff. You don't want to have to go shoot it all again, do you? That's why you need to think about how and how often you're going to back up your project—even if the plan ends up being "I don't care about it enough to bother."

Those $5 DVD-Rs, if you didn't know, can be used to store 4.7 GB of data files in lieu of video. So using the previous formula, a $5 disc can hold more than 20 minutes of high-quality video.

Give it some thought if any of your footage is worth protecting.

I'll talk more about backup options for huge projects in Chapter 8.

R.T.F.M. (Read the fine manuals)

Last but not least, before you begin the project, read the manual. Which one? Every one. With the exception of iDVD, this book isn't going to show you how to use anything—not iMovie or your camcorder or the new FireWire drive you just bought. So read their manuals before beginning your project, not in the middle when you're feeling pressured.

Whenever I hear someone say, "Mac users don't need to read manuals," I always correct them. Much of the power and elegance of today's Macintosh software is concealed, and if you don't read the documentation, you will no doubt miss out on powerful features that aren't in the menus. Even with simple programs like iDVD and iMovie.

Since neither iMovie nor iDVD comes with a printed manual, check out their tutorials and help systems. A camcorder may work fine in its fully automatic mode, but it could work much better using manual settings appropriately. You'll never know if you don't read the manual.

The better you know your tools, the better results you'll get. So just knuckle down and do it. Read the manuals and get to know your tools before you begin a project with any sort of deadline.

DVD Preproduction Checklist

- **Start Mac folder, notebook, or note file
  (or physical file folder)**

- **Define Five Ws**

  Who is the audience? Who are you making this
  project for?

  What is the purpose of this project?

  Where are the production facilities and locations for
  this project?

  When does it have to be completed?

  Why am I doing it?

- **Summarize project in one sentence**

- **Create road maps**

  Script

  Shot list

  Storyboards

  Schedule

  Budget

- **Further considerations**

  Locations

  Lighting

  'Lectricity

  Sound

- **Home on the Mac**

  Disk space

  RAM

  Software

  Backup plan

  R.T.F.M.s

Introduction to Making DVDs

It's time now for the moment you've been waiting for—making a DVD with iDVD. After the traditional brief introduction, we'll look at what it takes to create a DVD, but this time we'll do it tutorial-style.

Like the Apple iDVD tutorial that comes with iDVD (you *did* go through it, didn't you?), this chapter merely serves as an introduction to the program. But we'll actually roll up our sleeves and dig into iDVD itself, looking at the steps it takes to go from opening the program to clicking the Burn button. Then, the next chapter hardly talks about iDVD at all—it focuses on the things like shooting and editing that happen before you even fire up iDVD. After that, we'll get back to iDVD, looking more closely at importing files, creating menus and buttons, adding and managing audio, creating your own artwork, compression, and lots more.

There's a method to my madness. At least in theory, by the time we get to Chapter 5 (where we pick back up with iDVD—the program) and chapters beyond, you'll know just how all the pieces go together, and should have ideas about how you want to assemble and present them with iDVD.

iDVD: It's More Than Just a Program

Before we launch iDVD, let's look at the bigger picture and how the iDVD software fits into the DVD-making universe. Computers equipped with SuperDrives come with QuickTime, iMovie 2, and iDVD 2 pre-installed, so you have what you need to start making movies and DVDs (except for, perhaps, a digital camcorder) as soon as you unpack your new Mac and turn it on.

But making a DVD takes a bit more work than merely launching your copy of iDVD 2 and clicking a few times.

Actually, you probably could make a DVD just that easily. It might stink, but you could "make a DVD" with that little effort.

iDVD is more than just a program—it's a piece of Apple's cradle-to-grave integrated system for producing DVDs that you can view on most home DVD players. Because Apple makes everything in this DVD-making process—the hardware, software, operating system, video card, hard disk connection, motherboard, ROMs, and so on—Apple has much more control over how these elements work together than Dell or Gateway or any other Windows system manufacturer can ever have. But iDVD alone is not really enough to make a DVD.

I'm trying to say that DVDs will be much more interesting if you first edit all your raw footage with the included iMovie software from Apple. Or, if you have higher aspirations, you can edit video with a more capable, more expensive, nonlinear video editing program like Final Cut Pro (also from Apple), Adobe Premiere, or EditDV.

That's one of the beauties of iDVD—it doesn't care how you edit your video. As long as it's output as QuickTime, it'll work with iDVD.

The DVD standard requires that video files on DVDs be saved and compressed in the MPEG format. MPEG is a data format for compressing digital video into smaller files. And while that's really about all you need to know about it, I'd be remiss if I didn't tell you at least a little bit more. To wit: iDVD automatically converts your content (video, audio,

*stills, slideshows, and so on) into MPEG format before it
burns the disc. This conversion takes approximately one to
three times the length of the video segment, depending on
the speed of your Mac and the QuickTime compression
scheme used when the movie was originally saved.*

Here's another example of how iDVD is just part of a bigger
system: When you create a video DVD using iDVD you import
graphics files, video content, and audio tracks, all created by
other programs like Photoshop, Bias PEAK, GraphicConverter,
iMovie, iPhoto, or whatever program you prefer. Again, only
after creating all of your "elements" with other software do
you use iDVD to assemble those elements, and add menus,
buttons, slideshows, and other DVD features.

If you think back to the five phases of creating a DVD I mentioned in Chapter 1—plan, create, encode, author, and
record—you'll see that iDVD has little to do with the first two
steps. That's because—let's all say it together now: *iDVD 2 is
more than just a program—it's a piece of Apple's cradle-to-grave
integrated system for producing DVDs.*

iDVD 2: More Better Than Before

It seems unlikely that any of you are still using the first version of iDVD, but if you are, you
should get iDVD 2 immediately—it'll be the best $20 you spend on this whole endeavor. Not
just because it's the version this book is about, but because version 2 is faster than version 1
and includes many enhanced features.

To begin with, iDVD 2 provides an improved interface, comes with more and better templates,
and handles all the MPEG encoding and DVD disc formatting automatically in the background.

That's right: iDVD 2, bless its little heart, includes *background encoding*. As soon as you add a
movie to your DVD project, the MPEG encoding process starts in the background while you
continue working, which saves a significant amount of time when you burn the disc.

This is good. (And you have Mac OS X's robust multitasking support to thank for it.)

Finally, as if that weren't enough, iDVD 2 has nifty "motion menus." This means the menu
buttons on your DVDs can be movies, not merely still images or text, just like those fancy store-
bought DVDs from major studios. Sort of.

You can use the Apple templates (you'll see them in a few pages) or you can make your own
motion menus with iMovie 2 or another video editor and iDVD 2, as you'll see in Chapter 6.

If you don't already have it, you can get iDVD 2 (which comes on a DVD, not a CD, by the way)
from the Apple store online (http://store.apple.com) or by calling 1-800-MY-APPLE. The disc is
free but there is a shipping and handling charge (which was $19.95 when we went to press).

Don't panic. We'll be talking about output—compressing and saving and importing—soon, and it's not as geeky as it sounds here.

Still, you can't just launch iDVD and immediately turn out a studio-quality disc. There's much to be done before you use iDVD. In my opinion, it's much better to complete most (or all) of the video, audio, and still image elements before you even launch iDVD to put the finishing touches on the job.

Onward.

Importing and Encoding

Now that I've spent several pages explaining why you *don't* just jump into iDVD without creating some content first, that's exactly what I'm going to ask you to do.

You see, iDVD doesn't come with a manual, so Apple recommends you work your way through the included iDVD tutorial. It shouldn't take you more than an hour to complete, and it exposes you to many program features in a short time.

But I found that this tutorial is also short on explanations—it shows *what* to do, but it doesn't provide much detail about *why* you're doing it, or *other ways* of doing it.

That's what every hands-on tutorial in this book will be shooting for. And, in addition, the ones in this chapter are aimed at getting you familiar with iDVD's rich set of features.

Getting started

For this section, we're going to pretend you've already completed Steps 1 and 2—planning the project and creating the content elements. We'll be using the movies, pictures, and music you received with your copy of iDVD in the Tutorial folder to simulate those steps.

When you installed iDVD, the tutorial should automatically have been installed in a folder called "Tutorial" in your iDVD folder. If you can't find the Tutorial folder on your hard disk, try this: Choose iDVD Tutorial from the iDVD Help menu, then click the "Open the iDVD Tutorial project and continue" link at bottom left. If it doesn't find the Tutorial for you, you may have to reinstall the program. Also, if you've moved the iDVD folder (for example, put it in a subfolder of Applications), Help won't be able to find it.

Let's open that Tutorial project and get going. You can do this in either of two ways. Here's the first way:

1. Launch iDVD and choose iDVD Tutorial from the Help menu.

2. Click the "Open the iDVD Tutorial project and continue" link at bottom left.

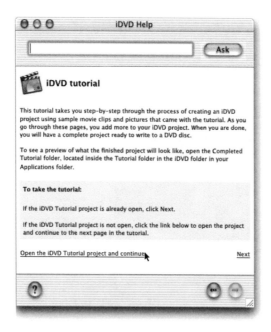

The second way is even simpler:

1. From the Finder, open the Start Here file in the Tutorial folder.

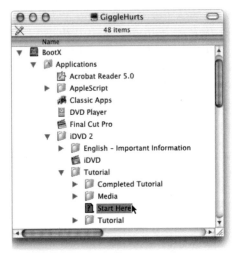

Whichever you do, when you're done, you should have two windows on your screen—the iDVD Help window and the South Pacific project window, as shown in **Figure 3.1**.

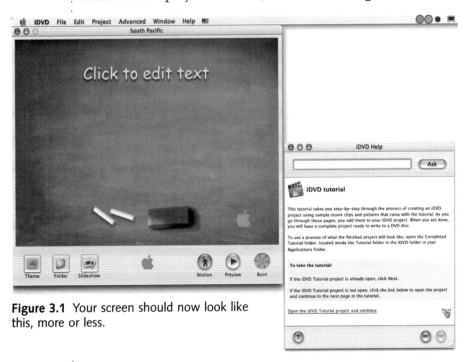

Figure 3.1 Your screen should now look like this, more or less.

Finally, click the *Next* link at the lower right of the iDVD Help window and you're ready to begin.

Importing (and encoding)

After you complete Steps 1 and 2 for your project, the next step is to import that content—your movies, still pictures, and sound files. That way, iDVD can begin encoding them in the background while you work on other things, as you'll see in a moment.

Right now, I want you to import at least one file so iDVD has something to chew on (encode in the background) while you continue to work on the rest of the tutorial.

This isn't a bad habit—importing your movies earlier rather than later. Compression takes quite a bit of time, so you might as well let the program get to work on that while you're doing other things.

The files you're going to use are in the Media folder, in the Tutorial folder, and are shown in **Figure 3.2.**

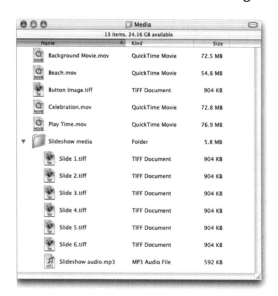

Figure 3.2 QuickTime movies, TIFF graphics, and MP3 audio are just some of the types of files you can use with iDVD.

You'll learn more than you want to know about file formats in Chapter 5.

We'll start with the file Background Movie.mov in the Media folder. Choose File > Import > Background Video and select the file. When it opens in iDVD, things should look something like **Figure 3.3.**

Figure 3.3
There's nothing fishy about having a movie playing in the background like this.

If your screen doesn't look like Figure 3.3, make sure you imported the correct file. Also make sure that you didn't choose Import > Video instead of Import > Background Video. They're not the same.

You should be seeing fish swim and hearing a sweet little jazz composition. If you're not (but your screen does look like Figure 3.3), click the Motion button.

Now, sit back for a second and admire your handiwork. You already have a background movie for your DVD. The excitement should last about 38 seconds, which is roughly the length of two repetitions of the movie (it loops automatically). When you begin to get sick of it, click the Motion button (again).

Notice how the background movie dims when you turn motion off; that's just one of iDVD's elegant touches.

Let's add a normal (non-background) movie. While you could choose Import > Video to do this, I find the drag-and-drop method easier. Just drag the movie file Celebration.mov onto the project in iDVD, like this:

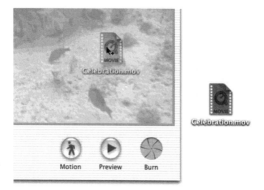

And when you release the mouse, you'll have created a movie button, as shown in **Figure 3.4**.

Figure 3.4 I know it doesn't look like much yet. But it will.

Import the other two tutorial movies, Beach.mov and Play Time.mov, using either method you know already. Let iDVD chew on them while you get to work on the next step, which is...

Authoring

Now it's time for what I consider the fun part: the authoring stage. I define this as, "everything you use iDVD for except burning." Since much of what you do in iDVD will change if you change your theme, let's start by looking at themes and how they work.

Themes—They're not just for songs and novels anymore

One of the best things about iDVD is the 14 included themes. These are professionally designed interface shells you fill with your own titles, movies, sounds, fonts, button shapes and styles, and almost every other visual element your DVD will present to the viewer.

But enough jabber. **Figure 3.5** shows what these lifesavers look like:

Figure 3.5 The iDVD themes look like this, only much more colorful.

I was hoping for something a little more elegant in the tutorial than the Chalkboard theme. Luckily, that's the whole point of having themes. To choose a new theme, open the Theme panel and select a theme. It couldn't be easier.

To open the Theme panel:

- Choose Show Theme Panel from the Project menu.
- Or use the keyboard shortcut Command-Shift-B.
- Or click the little Theme button.

Use one of those three methods now and the Theme panel will pop out of the left side of the main window, as you can see in **Figure 3.6.**

If you've done everything correctly thus far, your project should look like something like Figure 3.6 right now. If it doesn't, go back and reread the earlier sections to see if you can track down the place where you went astray.

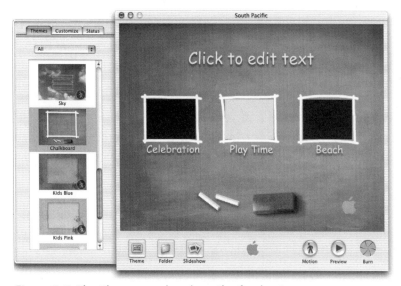

Figure 3.6 The Theme panel—where the fun begins.

I said I wanted elegant, so I scrolled up to the top of the list and selected the theme I consider iDVD's most beautiful, the Global theme, shown in **Figure 3.7.**

Figure 3.7 Beats the heck out of that fish thing, eh?

Try some of the other themes on for size—just click 'em in the Theme panel and take a peek. The ones with the little circle-dude in the lower right corner are motion menus. Be sure to turn them on by clicking the Motion button so you can enjoy the full effect.

When you've peeked all you're going to peek, choose the Global theme again so yours has at least some chance of looking like mine in the upcoming pictures.

Menus and buttons and text (oh my!)

Text in iDVD is as easy to deal with as Themes. To change button or menu text, just click the text to select it, like this:

Then type your replacement text, like this:

That's all there is to it. Feel free to change the title of your project or the title of any or all of the movies in the project now.

Next, let's see some motion buttons. When you add a movie to an iDVD project, the button created in the main window is automatically a motion-menu button. To see a preview of one now, click the Motion button.

By default, iDVD uses the first frame of the movie as its preview image. (If you've created a poster frame in your QuickTime movie, that frame will be used instead.)

To change the still image to another frame in the movie, drag the slider above it, as shown in **Figure 3.8.**

Figure 3.8
Notice how the picture changes when the slider above it slides.

If you want to *remove* the motion menu and use a still image on a button instead, just click the button to select it, move the slider to the frame you like best, then click the Movie check box above the slider to deselect it.

Add some pizzazz with a slideshow

If you have a digital still camera or your camcorder can take decent still pictures (most can't), the iDVD slideshow feature is a low-maintenance way to share lots of pictures and present them in a unique manner.

And, as always, iDVD's slideshow feature couldn't be easier to use. Just click the Slideshow button.

That will create a new My Slideshow button in your project.

Double-click it to open the slideshow editor window. Then drag the six pictures named Slide 1 through Slide 6 (from the Tutorial/ Media folder) to the slideshow window, as shown in **Figure 3.9.**

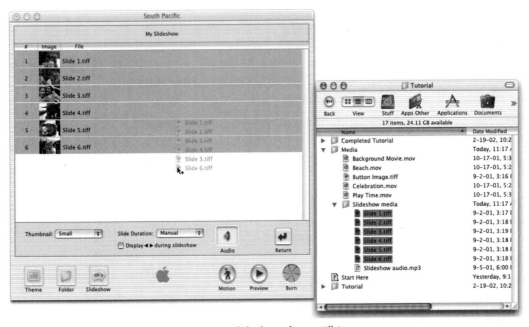

Figure 3.9 Yes, it is this easy to create a slideshow from still images.

Next we'll add background music by dragging the file Slideshow audio.mp3 into the Audio "well," like this:

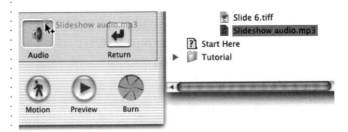

Other slideshow options include large or small thumbnail pictures (in the Thumbnail submenu), how long each slide remains on-screen (in the Slide Duration submenu), and whether or not the viewer can click the Next and Previous buttons on the DVD remote control to see the next or previous slide (the "Display during slideshow" check box). All of these items are shown in **Figure 3.10.**

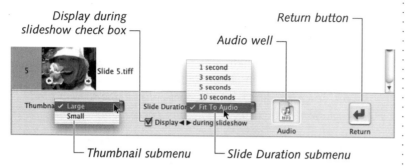

Display during
slideshow check box

Audio well

Return button

Thumbnail submenu

Slide Duration submenu

Figure 3.10 These are the other slideshow options.

Click the Return button, name your slideshow, and use the slider to choose a picture
to represent it, like this:

Now, let's take a quick look at how to finish things up, so we
can move on to the even better stuff.

The Grand Finale

At this point, imagine that our little project is as done as it's
going to get. Now there are only two things left to do—preview
it and burn it.

Not-so-sneaky Preview

At $5 a pop for blank DVD-R discs,
burning a disc with a mistake on it
can get real expensive real fast. Fortunately, the preview mode lets you catch
mistakes before you burn. Complete
with genuine simulated faux remote
control, the fabulous preview mode lets
you test your project before you click
the $5 Burn button.

To preview your project, click the
Preview button. Presto! It looks like
Figure 3.11.

Figure 3.11 Dig that
genuine simulated,
software-emulated
remote control!

To exit preview mode, click the Preview button again or click the Exit button on the faux remote.

If you have motion menus in your project, you must turn motion on before you click Preview or you won't see your motion menus. That's no big deal—just exit preview mode, click Motion to turn them on, then click Preview again.

But if you don't turn on motion before you burn a DVD, your disc will not have motion menus.

In preview mode, use the arrow buttons on the faux remote control to select a button on-screen, then click the Enter button to activate it.

You can also click a button on-screen directly with the Mac cursor to activate it in preview mode.

Use the Backward and Forward buttons on the faux remote for slideshows, like Figure **3.12.**

Figure 3.12
Click to advance to the next slide.

The arrow buttons on either side of the Enter button on the faux remote also serve as Backward and Forward buttons.

Finally, the Title and Menu buttons on the faux remote return you to the DVD's menu (Title always takes you to the "top" menu, and Menu takes you to the last menu you were in).

Although I saved the preview function until near the end of this chapter, you can preview your iDVD project at any time. In fact, it's probably a good idea to preview your project every now and then during the authoring phase. I switch back and forth often so I know how elements will look on a home DVD player and how they'll respond to clicks on the home DVD's remote control.

OK, you now know how to author with iDVD. Sure there are still a lot of cool things you haven't learned yet, like how to create your own themes or customize Apple's themes to your own tastes. And you'll learn that soon, but consider this: With what you know right now, you *could* burn a DVD that would impress 99 percent of the people who watch it.

> *Of course, since it only contains 90 seconds of video right now, they wouldn't stay impressed long. But they would almost certainly be impressed with your DVD-making skills.*

Burn, baby, burn

After you've gone through the preview-and-tweak cycle a few times, you're ready to burn your masterpiece onto a DVD-R disc.

> *Remember—DVD-R discs are write-once discs. Once you burn it, it's burnt. You can't change anything on that disc. If you make changes to your iDVD project, you have to burn a new $5 DVD-R disc. Try to avoid costly mistakes.*

Now I'm not saying you should waste a perfectly good DVD-R disc on the tutorials we just completed. But if you *did* want to burn one now, here's what you would do.

Click the Burn button once. It pulsates to let you know it's awake, as shown in **Figure 3.13.**

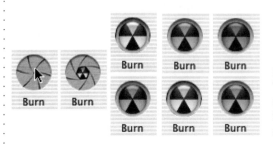

Figure 3.13
The click-and-pulsate effect, captured through the magic of stop-motion animation.

Click the Burn button again and one of two things will happen. Either this:

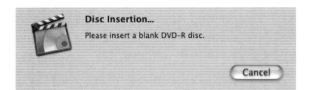

As I warned earlier, if you don't turn on motion before you burn a DVD, the DVD will not have motion menus. Now iDVD is warning you a second time. Click Cancel and turn on motion.

Or this:

Disc Insertion...
Please insert a blank DVD-R disc.

Cancel

This is it. If you insert a blank DVD-R disc now, the burning will happen. I'd like to tell you it happens immediately, but it doesn't. How long it takes from clicking Burn to playing the disc on the DVD player in the den depends on how much video is on the disc and the speed of your Mac. Apple says you can figure roughly 2 to 3 minutes of encode/burn time per minute of video on the DVD. So a DVD with 90 minutes of video on it (the maximum allowed), might take as long as 4.5 hours to encode and burn.

If your movies have been sitting in iDVD the whole time you've been working on this project, the encoding is already done. We'll talk more about encoding in Appendix B.

Remember, this chapter is merely a hands-on introduction. You're going to spend a lot more time customizing themes, menus, and buttons in upcoming chapters, but for now, you know enough to burn a decent disc if you had to. And enough to plan a more-than-decent disc if you wanted to.

And that's the end of that. Shall we move along now? It's time for tips, techniques, and advice about shooting and editing video for a DVD.

part 2

A Little Bit Beyond the Basics

Shooting and Editing Tips for Great Video

Now that you've seen just how easy it is to create a DVD with iDVD, let's take a look at how to create content and assemble it into a coherent movie.

Remember the five-step program I outlined in Chapter 1? Well, most of this chapter is about Step 2, creating. We'll look at things you can do when shooting and editing to get the best possible results. And we'll throw in a dash of Step 1, planning, to see what you can do *before* you shoot or edit to get the best possible results.

Even iDVD and iMovie can't work miracles. They can't overcome the GIGO (Garbage In, Garbage Out) effect—if you feed them lousy video and audio, you end up with lousy video and audio. In Hollywood, they often say, "It's OK; we'll fix it in post-production" (editing), but for mere mortals, it's better if you start with good raw material.

Shooting Better Movies

Before you shoot anything, become familiar with the operation of your camera, audio gear, lights, and other equipment. And, like a Boy Scout, be prepared for anything. So here are some before-the-shoot tips I find helpful.

- **Batteries:** One is never enough. And don't forget to charge 'em *all* up before you hit the road.

- **Tapes:** Have a spare tape or three handy. Don't wait to buy them on the way to the shoot. They're cheap and you'll use them, so have a few with you at all times.

- **Other stuff:** Don't forget the cables, adhesive tape, tools, extension cords, lights, microphones, props, and anything else you're likely to need "on location."

If you keep all of your gear in a bag, ready for action, you can just grab it and go. I keep my camcorder, spare batteries, tapes, and a small microphone in my small camera bag. I just carry the whole thing with me whenever I think I may see something worth shooting. If I need additional gear for a particular shoot, I have a rather large duffel bag I can lug instead.

Be smart. You'll regret it forever if you miss that once-in-a-lifetime great shot because you didn't have a tape or your only battery ran out of juice.

And that's the end of my little sermon.

Sounding off

Many new filmmakers make the mistake of thinking audio isn't as important as video, and that if you just point the camera at the action, the sound recorded through your camcorder's microphone will be good enough.

And it is, at least for some things. But even if it's a great mic, it's still attached to the camcorder. So, as I said in Chapter 2, if there's a lot of ambient noise or if your subject isn't near the camera or speaks quietly, the audio you record will suffer.

Some on-camera microphones pick up camera noise from the tape transport mechanism or zoom lens motor, too, so be careful of that if you're using the built-in mic.

Good sound gives you options; bad sound is hard to fix after the fact. Think of it this way: The sound can't possibly be too good, but it can easily be too bad. If you get good audio in the field, you'll have far more possibilities later when you edit and "sweeten" the audio.

Sweetening is post-production sound editing and mixing. Overdubs, narration, sound effects, background music, applause, and laugh tracks are all added during sweetening. It also refers to processing the sound tracks with filters, equalizers, or other devices, if necessary, to compensate for badly recorded field audio. In a nutshell, everything you do to the sound in post-production is "sweetening."

So how do you record field audio that sounds great? The first rule is to get the microphone as close to the speaker as possible.

By "speaker," I mean, of course, the person speaking. It's a bad idea to stick a microphone into the other kind of speaker (an electronic or electromagnetic device that reproduces sound). Unless you like the eardrum-shattering screech of feedback.

Second, most camcorders have a headphone jack. Use it. Get some headphones and start wearing them before you roll any tape, then keep them on while you shoot. Listen for buzzing, humming, and other types of interference as well as for natural sounds and sound levels. Electronic equipment, neon signs, and all kinds of other devices can wreak havoc with microphones. If you don't listen, you won't know...at least not until it's too late.

Mister Microphone

The key to capturing good live audio is to use the right microphone for the job. Don't rely on your camcorder's built-in mic for critical audio. Even an inexpensive mic, if placed properly, will do a better job.

There are several types of microphone. Here's a quick run-down designed to help you choose the one (or more) that will be most useful to your shooting style.

A *cardioid* microphone has a heart-shaped pickup pattern that is more sensitive to sound coming from the front and sides than sound coming from behind. Here's my rendition of what a cardioid mic and its pickup pattern look like:

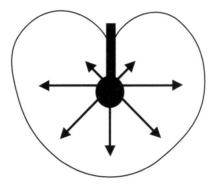

If extraneous noise is a concern, a *directional microphone* is an option. Directional mics have a focused pickup pattern. An extreme example is a *shotgun* mic, which has a long, narrow, tightly-focused pickup pattern, like this:

Super-cardioid mics are a versatile type of directional mic, and may be what came mounted on your camcorder. Their pickup pattern looks something like this:

Then there are *omni-directional* microphones, which pick up sound from all directions equally, like this:

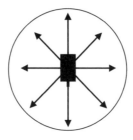

Many lavaliere and clip-on microphones are omni-directional. In spite of that, because you can place them close to the speaker's mouth, they're an excellent choice in difficult situations where ambient noise or other sounds might ruin a shot.

You might also consider a *boom,* the fishing-pole-like contraption that lets you dangle the microphone just out of the shot. Sometimes nothing else will do.

Many good microphones come with foam covers, often gray in color, that look like head covers for golf clubs. Although they do provide some protection, they're actually windscreens, and can filter out wind and breathing noises.

Use them even when there's no wind—they also suppress sibilance and popped Ps in speech.

Ready, Steady, Go

We've all seen home movies where the picture jumps around as the cameraperson (bless their heart) walks around obliviously, swinging the camera hither and yon, bobbing and weaving like Muhammad Ali in his heyday. So unless you're filming a documentary about an earthquake, you know to avoid jittery scenes and poorly framed shots.

Without spending big bucks for a camera stabilizer unit like the Steadicam shown in **Figure 4.1,** there are a few things you can do if you absolutely must move the camera while tape is rolling.

Figure 4.1 Steadicam is the inventor and maker of camera stabilizing systems like this one.

The Steadicam and other external stabilizing devices are expensive—hundreds or thousands of dollars. But if your material demands the camera be in motion, these devices open up a whole world of possibilities. Of course, if you're shooting home movies, they're overkill. They take quite a bit of time to master, too, so don't buy one the day of the shoot.

One inexpensive way to minimize jumpiness is the "poor man's Steadicam," otherwise known as a tripod. Tripods are widely available, and prices start well under $100. If you can use a tripod for a particular shot, you should. The resulting video will look much more professional. A tripod won't help for fancy stuff like "follow shots," or "crane shots," but you can pan or tilt if you must (remember to do it slowly and smoothly).

Though they cost a bit more, a tripod with a "fluid head" will pan and tilt more smoothly than a cheapie.

If you don't have a tripod, but don't need to move the camera, look for a solid surface to lean against—a tree, table, fence, rail, low wall, car hood, or whatever. When working tripod-free, you should stabilize the camera with a stationary object whenever you can.

If you aren't using a tripod and you have to move the camera while tape's rolling, be very aware of the camera and its position. Move as smoothly and slowly as you can, with your elbows locked to your sides to provide additional stabilization. With practice, you can minimize most camera jitter and jumpiness, and you may even develop a usable style.

There is a "hand-held" look that can be used (sparingly) to great effect. Watch for it in independent film productions, true-crime television shows, and music videos. While this effect is often achieved by using a Steadicam or other hardware, with a little practice, you should be able to do a fair approximation.

Zoom-zoom

Another way to make your footage look better is to keep your finger off the darn Zoom button. Unless you're attempting the psychedelic look, don't zoom when you can avoid it.

Rapid, repeated zooming could give your viewers vertigo. You don't want to make Great Aunt Mabel toss her cookies.

Of course there are exceptions. Sometimes it's necessary to do a lot of zooming (sporting events, kids playing, and so forth). If you're shooting something or someone from some distance, you can zoom in until the subject is framed the way you like. And if you must zoom, zoom slowly if you plan to use the zooming part in your movie. Later you can edit out the zoom part or not.

Finally, if your camcorder offers both optical and digital zoom, turn off the digital zoom if you can—it will only cause you heartache. Because it uses interpolation to "guess" what the way far away object actually looks like, the digital zoom introduces noise and artifacts that leave you with an unidentifiable blob where you thought the subject was. So just turn it off and forget you have it.

For the most part go easy on the zoom. And when you're editing, consider every zoom on the tape a prime candidate for cutting.

Night and Day

As I said back in Chapter 2, the better the lighting, the better your footage will look. It's true that you frequently have little or no control over lighting—when you're shooting outdoors, for example. But anything you shoot in a place with lights and electricity (even your kid's birthday party) can be improved by lighting. And even when you can't control the lighting, your end result will almost always improve if you know where your light source is and position the camera to take advantage of it.

The best situation for controlled lighting is a soundstage, like those used by TV news shows and the like. While you may never shoot on a soundstage, knowing a few "rules" for lighting one can help you in other situations.

On a soundstage you can place a light almost anywhere you like. When you have this kind of flexibility, you should have at least two light sources (three or four is even better). Your primary light source, sometimes called a *key light*, should be positioned above and slightly to one side of your camera—left or right, it's your choice. Most lighting guides suggest that the light be positioned at a 45-degree angle from the subject and at a 45-degree angle from the ground.

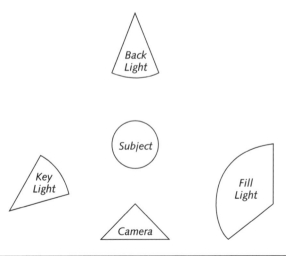

Outside, the sun can often fill the role of key light, but be careful about sun or other bright light shining directly in your subjects' faces. For one thing, you risk overexposure, which can make things look faded or bleached. For another, you usually don't want your actors squinting painfully into the camera.

Soft light is your friend; harsh light is your nemesis. Direct light is very hard to photograph well on tape. Bounce light off the walls or ceiling, reflect it off white card stock, or drape it with something, but try not to use direct lighting when you can avoid it.

Your goal should be to throw enough light on the subject to provide the camera a clear, sharp image without glare or shadows. Some of the tools you might use are *fill lighting, back lighting,* and *background lighting.*

A fill light is typically positioned on the opposite side of the camera from the key light. Its function is to eliminate shadows on the subject, such as those produced by the bill of a cap or by facial contours.

A back light is positioned behind your subject to isolate it from the background.

Background lighting shines on your background or backdrop. This is particularly useful when you have a dull, solid-colored wall as the background. Position the light below and behind your subject so that it projects up and onto the background.

> *Lighting is an art and there's no way I can do more than scratch the surface here. Mostly you'll learn by doing, but if proper video lighting interests you, there are entire books about it, as well as Web sites chock-full of information, discussions, and tips. You can use your favorite search engine with terms like "video production," "movie lighting," "key light," "fill light," and so on. I just tried it on Google (www.google.com), and the first page of results had half a dozen sites that looked useful to me.*

R.T.F.M.

Just in case you skipped that section of Chapter 2, "RTFM" is the commonly used acronym for "read the fine manual." Reading the instruction manual for your camcorder is not optional. But I've found that most people just skim it. So do yourself a favor and read it from cover to cover right now. I'll wait.

If you don't understand how the features on your camera work, you can't possibly configure it for the best results, and you may (albeit accidentally) change a setting and ruin a shot.

Note that many camcorders offer "presets" that adjust several settings at once for particular conditions. For example, my Canon ZR25 offers these six presets:

- Auto (camera does everything automatically)
- Sports (for clear images of fast-moving subjects)
- Portrait (for non-moving subjects in controlled-lighting situations)
- Spotlight (for live performances on a brightly lit stage)
- Sand & Snow (compensates for bright background)
- Low Light (for dimly lit scenes)

These presets are a good baseline, and many casual camcorder users never move beyond them. But if you understand the adjustments they make, you'll know how to make further adjustments manually if you wish, and you'll have much greater control over your work.

While a complete review of camcorder features is beyond this book's purview, at the very least you should know and understand the white balance, shutter speed, iris control, auto focus, and digital effects features (assuming your camera offers them).

White Balance: White-balancing your camera automatically filters out some color casts. If your camera has white-balance adjustment, read your manual and use it as instructed.

The human eye filters out color casts associated with different types of light: sunlight is typically bluish, incandescent lighting has a yellowish tinge, and fluorescent lighting has a greenish cast. You may not see it, but the camera records it, so get into the habit of white-balancing your camera before you begin rolling tape in a new environment or what you capture on tape may not look as you expect.

Shutter Speed: In a nutshell, faster speeds freeze action better but require more light; slower speeds may blur moving objects but require less light. Manually adjusting the shutter speed provides more flexibility than presets. If you have it, learn how to use it.

Iris Control: The camera attempts to adjust the iris (the opening) automatically when you have both dark and light areas in a shot—dark skin with white hair or shirt, a spot-lit performer on a dark stage, a dark-haired bride in a white dress, or even if you pan from light to dark or vice versa. As the iris adjusts, the scene will darken and brighten. It looks dorky. The manual iris control lets you compensate for this and capture cleaner footage.

Auto Focus: Most camcorders have this, but I think it looks like amateur night in Dixie and I hate the whine of its little motor (which the built-in microphone sometimes picks up, by the way).

Turning off Auto Focus makes it much more challenging to pan, tilt, zoom, and perform other camera moves. In addition, you may need to keep the subject in focus manually (or not, if that's the effect you're going for).

Digital Effects: Finally, avoid your camcorder's built-in digital effects—fade, wipe, dissolve, sepia, and all the rest. You can do the same things in iMovie, with more control and the Undo command. There's no way to undo effects created "in camera," they're applied to the tape immediately, like it or not. So add your effects in post-production, where you can remove them at will; don't apply them in the camera, where you'll be stuck with them forever.

Not-So-Obscura Camera Technique

Again, there's enough to say about filming technique to fill a whole book or two, and many authors have. That said, here are a few things I've learned as I've gotten more and more involved in video and filmmaking.

As I said before, zooming in or out alters the focus of your scene (the field of view changes along with the size of the subject). Here's a technique for keeping your subject in focus:

1. Turn off auto focus.

2. Zoom in on the subject.

3. Focus manually.

4. Zoom out without changing the focus.

When you zoom in with tape rolling, your subject will stay in perfect focus with none of the flickering and twitching auto focus would have caused.

Auto focus tries to home in on the closest object, so it gets twitchy when the subject of your scene is not the object closest to the camcorder. Auto focus may also freak out if your subject blends into the background. If you see this happening in the viewfinder/monitor, turn auto focus off and do it manually as described above.

An added benefit of manual focus is more control over depth of field, so you can blur an object in the foreground purposely, or focus tightly on something in the foreground with the background blurred. Experiment with these effects; they can give your video a more professional look.

You should think about editing as you shoot, and make sure you get enough *coverage* (different types of shots) to stitch together the scene you envision. A common and effective style is to set up a scene with a wide shot (one from a distance), then cut to medium, then to close-up, and alternate between medium and close-up from that point, maybe going to a wide shot at the end of the scene.

When you shoot on location, capture a few minutes of ambient noise and visuals. Shoot signs, buildings, doorways, windows, cars, people, and everything else, from various angles. Using editing tricks you'll learn a little later, these snippets may be just what you need to make a sequence really shine.

Keep your composure

In still photography and paintings, it has long been accepted that you should center the subject in the frame. This is a bit of an oversimplification. A better rule is to imagine a tic-tac-toe grid over your subject and use the four line intersections to position the focal point.

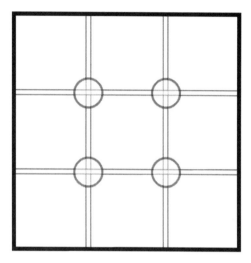

Cinematographers call this *composition* and it's yet another thing to think about as you plan and shoot your video.

It's often more interesting to compose a picture (or frame) with the focal point off-center, like this:

A composition with the subject plopped right in the middle, like this, can be dull:

Our good friend, artist Sharon Steuer, created a fantasy composition for my wife and I. Notice that at least two focal points are near corners and none are smack dab in the middle in this example:

We've all seen pictures where some kid sticks his fingers up behind somebody's head like horns, or where it looks like something in the background is growing out of the subject. This is what happens when you ignore the background when setting up a shot. In filming, as in still photos, pay attention to the background and its relation to your subject. In a studio setting you can adjust the background or the lights, but in more casual settings, the solution may be to reposition the camera or shoot from a different angle.

Camera angle is another weapon in your arsenal—the camera's position relative to your subject. The corny old method of walking around framing the shot through a rectangle formed by your thumbs and index fingers actually works. You can go high-tech by using your camcorder's LCD screen for the same purpose, but I don't feel that gives quite as much control over the framing of the shot. And you don't get to look like you're Cecil B. De Mille.

Vertical camera angle also has an impact. You might want to have a stool handy: Stand on it to shoot slightly downward or sit on it for an upward angle. You'll find your scenes of kids or dogs are much more interesting if you're down at their eye level, rather than hovering above them shooting downward.

While you're thinking about your coverage, try to get additional takes from different angles and distances if you can reshoot scenes. When you edit your movie, you can use clips from different perspectives to create a more compelling result. For long scenes like a graduation or a recital, move around and film portions of the event from different locations. If you can have two or three takes of a scene, you can also pick and choose portions of each clip to avoid flubbed lines (or save the outtakes for a blooper reel, if your sense of humor follows that bent).

You can learn a lot about camera position and movement by watching TV and movies. Turn down the audio, ignore the story line, and concentrate on where the camera is and what it's pointed at (a.k.a. the "cinematography").

One last bit of advice before we move along to the editing phase. Before you start to record the real thing, record a short test shot and play it back with your headphones on so you can hear it, too. I just know you'd hate to record 30 minutes of award-winning footage and then find out that the microphone wasn't completely plugged in and you have no sound, or that your finger was covering the lens, or, well, you get the picture.

Editing with iMovie 2

Though I do know what happens when I make an assumption, I'm going to assume here that you're using iMovie 2 to edit and prepare your video. After all, I know you have a copy (it's preinstalled on every Mac that has iDVD) and it's designed to work seamlessly with iDVD. So if you're using a more powerful editing program, bear with me.

If you're a Final Cut Pro user, I recommend the Final Cut Pro Visual QuickPro Guide *from Peachpit Press (this book's publisher). I've made a lot of movies with FCP and found this book really helpful. Also, Scott Smith has written two excellent books for fledgling filmmakers—*Making iMovies *and* FireWire Filmmaking *(both, not coincidentally, from Peachpit Press). If you want to know more about making better movies on your Mac than I can possibly tell you in this chapter, either or both will serve you well.*

iMovie may be the easiest video-editing software ever made. That's both its blessing and its curse. A blessing, because anyone who can use a FireWire cable can import video and start creating movies. A curse, because anyone with a FireWire cable can create movies and distribute them—on DVD or CD-ROM, by email, Web streaming, or who knows what else. If you haven't seen any yet, be prepared to see some really awful video.

Maybe you aren't old enough to remember the early days of desktop publishing, when user-selectable fonts in printed documents were a novelty. Believe me when I tell you I saw lots of incredibly ugly "ransom note" documents, with five or six fonts, multiple font sizes and colors, and every available style. Trust me on this one: Ugly video is going to make desktop publishing faux pas seem quaint by comparison.

Since iMovie 2 is so easy to use and the tutorial teaches the basics so well, in this section I'll focus on making the most of iMovie. We'll look at some things you can do with iMovie as well as some things you should probably avoid doing (or overdoing).

Effective effects

Version 2 of iMovie includes a number of professional-looking special effects to help you enhance your movies. And these effects are truly special—they're a lot like the ones you see on TV and in motion pictures. If you use them tastefully, you can make your productions look ever so professional. But use them inappropriately or overuse them and you'll have a ransom-note video that screams "amateur."

As with fonts in publications, less is more when adding effects. Don't overuse them. Just because they're there doesn't mean you have to use them. If your movie is nothing but effects, they lose their effectiveness. Or make people queasy. But judicious use can make your movie more effective, not to mention slicker-looking.

Now that you've been warned, let's look at some of the effects in iMovie's Effects panel.

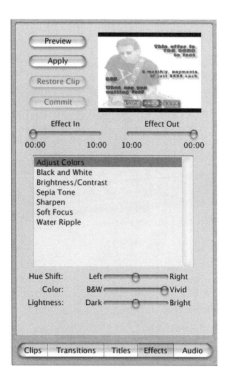

Click the Effects button at the bottom of the shelf (it's highlighted in the picture above) to get to them.

Effects are applied to clips selected in the Clip Viewer or Timeline, not clips on the shelf.

You can apply effects in this panel to all or part of a clip. Play around with them until you get the hang of it.

Some of the effects take a while to apply. When an effect is being applied, you'll see a small, red bar with progress numbers on the selected clip in the Clip Viewer. This is the progress indicator showing how far iMovie has gotten in applying your effect (136 out of 680 frames). I know it looks gray in the picture, but the numbers and the line below them are fire-engine red on-screen.

Transitions

Transitions are a type of visual effect usually used between scenes or shots to link them together. In iMovie they're found in the Transitions panel. Click the Transitions button at the bottom of the shelf (it's highlighted in the picture below) to get to them.

To move from scene to scene, consider simple "cuts," with no effects at all. That's right. You don't have to have a transition each time a clip starts or ends. If you don't add a transition, all you have is a cut. And much of the time, a cut is all you should use.

That said, fading in and out of scenes is dramatic and effective, and appropriate for many transitions.

Like almost everything that can be cool and useful, transitions are frequently overused and abused. Go easy. A nice little fade in at the start or a fade out at the end will lend your movie a professional touch. But using every transition in the list in the first 2 minutes of your movie proclaims, "I'm a newbie!"

When you fade out from one scene then fade in to the next, it can be a beautiful thing. The cross dissolve, which is similar to fading in/out, is also appropriate for many transitions.

> *Try a long cross dissolve with slow-motion action footage on both sides. It'll remind you of every treacle-dripping sports movie you've ever suffered through.*

Some of the other transitions, though, such as push and scale down, should be reserved for special cases where you're trying to achieve a specific effect. For example, push works quite well as the transition effect for a slideshow. In my humble opinion, scale down only works if you're going for a sci-fi or psychedelic effect.

> *Speaking of which, you don't have to use video to use iMovie, you know. It's also swell for bringing still pictures to life, with music, even. I rarely use PowerPoint for this kind of slideshow, since iMovie lets me do more and my slideshows look better.*

Although you'll find that the fade in, fade out, and cross dissolve are most useful and most useable, even they can be overused. Remember the words of my great-uncle Yogi LeVitus: "Less is more. Unless you're talking food or beer."

Titles (or How to use text on-screen to win friends and influence people)

With iMovie 2, it's incredibly easy to add title screens, opening or closing credits, and captions or subtitles to your movie. A variety of title effects, including some that are very professional-looking, are available (where else?) in the Titles panel.

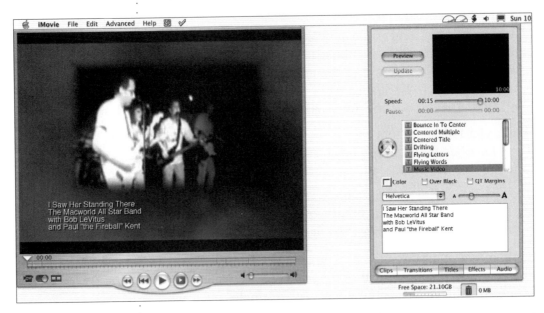

I'm partial to making music video parodies, so I'm a big fan of the Music Video title style, as shown above. But there are lots of other styles to imitate. You've all seen movies and TV shows where the actor's name appears as the actor first appears on-screen. This is a time-honored technique (albeit oft-overused) to introduce the cast, and it's easily recreated in iMovie.

If you're a fan of *JAG* or *The X-Files,* you'll probably love using the Typewriter style to introduce your scenes, as shown in **Figure 4.2.**

Add a typewriter sound for the full effect (it's a cliché, but an effective one).

Figure 4.2 The *X-Files*–style typewritten title card looks like it's being typed on the screen in real time.

To the folks involved in your magnum opus, the credits are often more important than the movie. You can create a very professional-looking set of opening credits using the Centered Multiple title style. You create pairs of lines and each pair will fade out to be replaced by the next pair fading in, as shown in **Figure 4.3.**

Figure 4.3 The Centered Multiple style has each name fade in, then out, followed by the next name, which fades in, then out.

The traditional closing credits are a rolling list with the character or job on the left and the individual on the right. Rolling Centered Credits (see **Figure 4.4**) and Rolling Credits will both do the job.

Figure 4.4 Rolling Centered Credits such as these are a good choice for closing credits.

Mixing several title effects tastefully can also provide attractive results. You can, for example, create multiple Drifting titles (in alternating directions) that appear in sequence. The downside of this method is that, since each title is rendered independently, you must drag each one to the Clip Viewer for rendering before you can start setting up the next one in the Title panel.

Each title has to be completely rendered before you can add the next credit, with one exception. When you check the Over Black option, you can just keep dragging them onto the Timeline or Clip Viewer, because the rendering is instantaneous. And white titles on a plain black background look elegant and professional.

Narration, sound effects, and background music

I can't overemphasize how important sound is to your movie. Recording sound in the field is merely the tip of the iceberg. Your soundtracks can be more than just the audio your camcorder recorded. You can add music, sound effects, and voiceovers to spice up even the most mundane footage. Just use your imagination.

iMovie includes a handful (if you have really small hands) of relatively useful sound effects.

Cat Meow	00:18
Crickets	06:04
Crowd Applause	06:11
Crowd Clapping	04:26
Dog Bark	01:24
Drum Roll	03:12
Footsteps	06:24
Forest Rain	05:04
Glass Breaking	02:07
Horn Honk	00:14
Horse Whinny	02:13
Kid Laugh	02:03
People Laugh	03:14
Thunder	06:01
Wagon Crash	03:16
Water Lapping	05:08
Whistle Up	02:04
Wild Laugh	04:08

Fortunately, those nice folks in Cupertino will give you hundreds or thousands of sound clips, music clips, and more, all absolutely free, just for making the right choice in computer platforms. Poke around the iMovie section of the Apple Web site at www.apple.com/imovie. I just downloaded 33 MB of choice sound effects to enhance my library, as shown in **Figure 4.5.**

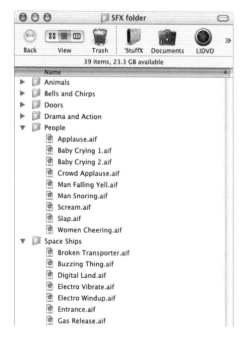

Figure 4.5
Just look at all these useful sound effects I got for free from Apple.

But wait: There's more. If you look on your iDisk, you'll find Apple has graciously provided you with a selection of more than 2,000 royalty-free songs in 35 genres, with most offered in 120, 60, 30, 20, 15, and 10 second versions.

This is an awesome deal. To get yours, open your iDisk, and follow the path shown in **Figure 4.6** (/Software/Extras/FreePlay Music/).

Figure 4.6 The FreePlay Music collections are a wonderful (and free) resource.

Add these songs in iMovie 2's Audio panel, shown in **Figure 4.7.** You'll find the short ones work nicely under titles, and the longer pieces can take you through an entire scene or sequence.

Many more sounds and songs can be purchased from killersound (www.killersound.com), Sounddogs (www.sounddogs.com), and others. But the FreePlay Music is a great start and you can't beat the cost. Zilch.

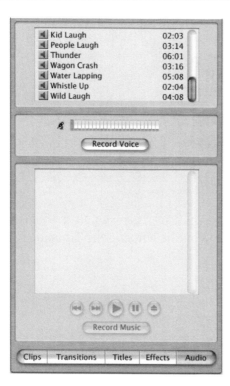

Kid Laugh	02:03
People Laugh	03:14
Thunder	06:01
Wagon Crash	03:16
Water Lapping	05:08
Whistle Up	02:04
Wild Laugh	04:08

Record Voice

Record Music

Clips | Transitions | Titles | Effects | Audio

Figure 4.7
Where the audio magic happens... audiomagically.

With an external microphone or your Mac's built-in mic (if it has one), you can add your own narration. And as long as you're not making a commercial movie or one that will be widely displayed, you can record tracks directly off your favorite audio CDs, too.

If you're going to record narration, speak slowly and distinctly. Your "normal" speaking cadence will probably sound rushed and lack clarity.

A Few More Neat Techniques

I've made quite a few QuickTime movies in my lifetime and have, over the years, discovered a few neat tricks and techniques I use as often as taste and good sense allow. Here they are.

Slo-mo and its obverse

Slow-motion and fast-motion photography are techniques that have been around since time immemorial. Or at least since movies were invented.

Surprisingly, iMovie isn't as forthcoming about how to do this as it could be. You see, the command isn't on any of the menus, and if you're using the Clip Viewer...

Well, it's not there either. The trick is to switch to the Timeline first. Just click the clock tab on the left, and the Timeline replaces the Clip Viewer.

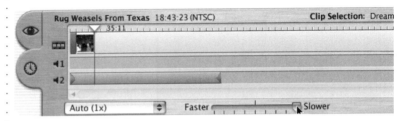

Move the slider left to make the selected clip run faster or to the right to make it slower.

Unlike the effects in the Effects panel, which can be applied to a portion of a clip in the Monitor window, these two effects—fast and slow motion—apply to the whole clip.

The workaround if you want to speed up or slow down part of a clip is to position the playhead where you want the slow or fast motion to start or end, and then choose Split Video Clip at Playhead from the Edit menu (or use the shortcut, Command-T). Now apply the speed change to the proper piece of clip.

Remember it's there, it's free, and it's quite flexible. You can slow down or speed up a scene or part of a scene a little or a lot. My kids love seeing themselves playing ball (basket, base, kick, soccer, foot, or other) in what I call, "Super-Duper-Slow-Mo." It's nothing more than iMovie's slowest setting, but the effect is dramatic and, if done tastefully (the way I always do it, of course), cinematic.

If you're going to apply other effects and a speed change to a clip, apply all the other effects first. When you apply an effect from the Effects panel to a clip (or a part of a clip), the clip's speed reverts to normal.

The audio philes

Some useful effects can only be achieved by mastering the Extract Audio command in the Advanced menu (or its shortcut, Command-J). This little gem separates a clip's video and audio tracks, as shown in **Figure 4.8**.

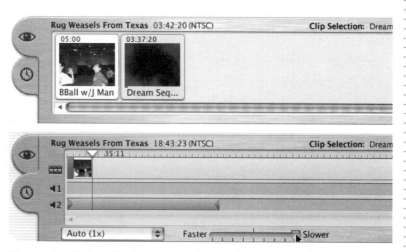

Figure 4.8 Before (top) and after (bottom) extracting the audio from the Dream clip.

You can then adjust the volume, fade in and out, or replace all or part of it. There are so many possibilities—you can even use the sound track from one clip to replace the sound track in another clip.

This can be a great solution when you have a good-looking clip that sounds bad or has some other audible problem.

Throw in the Split Selected Audio Clip at Playhead command (in the Edit menu, or use its shortcut, Command-T) and the Fade In and Fade Out controls, and you can do some fairly sophisticated stuff with sound. For example, if you want to have the music sound track fade out while the voices from the clip on-screen fade in, you *crossfade* from sound track to sound track using the Fade In and Fade Out controls, like this:

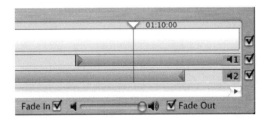

You can have your narration fade away as the music swells and the credits fill the screen. I'm telling you, the things you can do with these audio features alone...

OK. One last smart audio trick and we'll call it a day.

My friend Dennis Cohen, who helped me out with this chapter, says the pros call this little technique an *L-cut*. If you squint, the audio track (at the bottom) is longer than the video track above it, giving an L-shaped appearance in the Timeline, like this:

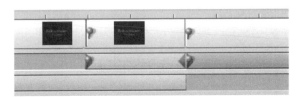

In this instance, the bottom sound track is the music that accompanies the first clip. That sound continues to play along with the audio from second clip (the top sound track). Here's how to do it with two adjacent clips in the Timeline:

1. Extract the audio from both clips. The first clip must have audio; it's OK if the second clip doesn't.

2. Lock both audio tracks to the start of their video tracks (you'll see little red push-pins after you do).

3. Select the first video clip and delete a portion from the end by using crop markers in the Monitor and choosing Edit > Clear or Edit > Cut. The amount of video you remove is the amount by which the second

clip's video will overlap the first clip's audio track. It should look something like this:

If you want both audio tracks to play simultaneously throughout the second clip, you're done. But if you want to trim away some or all of the audio from either clip, you certainly can. Tweak it until it sounds perfect to you. Congratulations. You now know how to assemble an L-cut, just like the pros do.

You can, obviously, do it in reverse, with the audio from the second clip beginning before the first clip ends. Not surprisingly, that is called a J-cut.

Here's a little example from a movie I just finished.

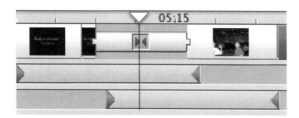

Video: The first clip is the opening title sequence. The middle item (where the playhead is resting) is a Cross-Dissolve transition. The second clip is sports footage of my son Jacob.

Audio: The music (top audio track—Survivor's "Eye of the Tiger," in case you were wondering) begins when the title clip starts and plays until the transition is over and then a few more frames. The basketball audio, on the bottom audio track, starts before the titles are done and plays through the transition, getting louder and louder until it dominates over the music. It looks and sounds like real television. And it never fails to impress those unfortunate enough to try this on a PC running Windows.

Onward!

Getting Your
Stuff into iDVD

If you have your project planned out—whether you're documenting your brother's wedding, reliving your vacation to the depths of Death Valley, or putting together instructional materials for co-workers—it's high time to get started making your own unique DVD. Some of the steps overlap with the sample DVD you made in Chapter 3, but this time I'll show you how to deal with situations that the quick tutorial doesn't cover and I'll show you how to turn your DVD into a highly customized project that you will truly be proud of.

The first steps, even before you open iDVD, are to collect your *assets* (images and video for now; I'll cover everything you need to know about sound in Chapter 7), make sure the files are in the right format, and map out where you want your slideshows and movies to go in your DVD.

We'll start with a quick look at each of these steps, then the excitement begins—importing your masterpieces into iDVD.

Don't worry yet about putting a pretty face on your DVD. Yet. You're going to get to make that DVD look just the way you want in Chapter 6.

First, Get Your Assets Together

Before you can import a single image or video, everything needs to be in just the right file format. Chances are, your images are already in the right format since iDVD will accept any Quick-Time-compatible still-image file.

> *For graphic images, that means you can format them as TIFF, PICT, JPEG, or any other QuickTime format.*

I use TIFF because it's a "lossless" format and I figure I never want to throw away information I may need later.

> *That doesn't mean you should comb your hard disk and change all of your images to TIFF. It's best to leave them alone if they're already in one of the other QuickTime formats. Every time you compress or re-save a file with compression, you take away resolution that can never be put back.*

As a rule, you always want to use the best or highest-quality source material you have and let any degradation come from iDVD's compression when you burn the disc. After all, if you give iDVD a pixelated, overly compressed JPEG file, for instance, iDVD isn't going to make it look *better*, if you know what I mean.

The same rule about choosing a format holds true for video—iDVD will accept almost any QuickTime-compatible video file (except QuickTime VR, MPEG-1, and formats with sprites). But that doesn't mean all video formats are created equal, at least not in the eyes of iDVD. You'll get the best results if you export your video in the DV stream format. To do that in iMovie, for instance, select Export Movie from the File menu. Then choose For iDVD from the Export To pop-up menu.

> *For the best results, Apple recommends using a video frame rate of 29.97 frames per second, no compression for audio, and an audio rate of 48 kHz. That's probably what your DV camcorder outputs, so don't worry too much about it.*

If you'll be sending your DVD across the briny seas—to Europe, that is—make sure you use the right format for videos. Since our Euro-pals have tellies that use the PAL format rather than NTSC, you must export your movies from your video-editing software in PAL format with a frame rate of 25 fps. Before you import them into iDVD, choose Preferences from the iDVD menu, and select the PAL option, as shown in **Figure 5.1.**

For more about video standards, formats, and compression in general, see Appendix B.

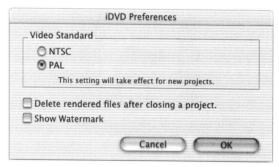

Figure 5.1 It's important to let iDVD know if you want to use the PAL format before you start your iDVD project or you'll have to start over from scratch.

Resolution also matters. The ideal size for graphic images is 640 x 480 pixels. If the images have a different proportion, a couple of things can go wrong: Either the images won't fill up an entire menu or button, leaving you with undesirable black bars to fill the empty space; or iDVD will resize the image, making it distorted or pixelated. To make your images fit the DVD window exactly, use a photo-editing application to resize the image to 640 x 480. For use as a button, any width and height with a 4:3 ratio will work.

Nobody wants a squashed ancestor, but that's just what I got for importing a wrong-sized graphic into iDVD:

That's supposed to be my infamous uncle Yogi LeVitus, who once said, "Don't squish my picture if you can avoid it."

Sometimes iDVD displayed this image with black bands on either side:

Neither of these alterations is what I wanted. So I put the image of Uncle Yogi back into my image editor (Photoshop 7, if you must know) and resized it to 640 x 480. That made Uncle Yogi look just right:

For video, the ideal size is 720 x 480 pixels. If you import video that's smaller than the standard DVD size of 720 x 480 (NTSC) or 720 x 576 (PAL), iDVD will scale it to fit the DVD window, which will almost certainly worsen the image quality.

One last detail to check before you import any images into iDVD is whether your images are oriented correctly. Be sure to flip any images in your image editor that are horizontal so that they don't lie sideways in your DVD.

Gather Your Images

Chances are, your images and movies are spread all over your hard drive in various folders. To make it easier to stay organized, make backing up your project as quick as possible, and even speed up burning the DVD, move all of your assets into one folder. That's where you'll want to keep your iDVD project file as well, once you create it.

Keep in mind that you don't have to create every bit of the content that will go on your DVD. Let's say at the last minute you wish you had a beautiful sunset to use as the backdrop on a secondary menu, but you don't have any decent sunset shots from your own collection of photos. Don't despair—the Internet is your friend in these desperate moments. There are plenty of sites that supply absolutely free images as long as you're not using them for commercial purposes. (If you do want to use them commercially, you'll have to get permission for copyrighted materials.)

Free Graphics.com (www.freegraphics.com) has a database of sites with images that are free for the taking. If you want the best that a little money can buy, take a look at the royalty-free images at Corbis's site (www.corbis.com). There are plenty of beautiful images in the $50 range. The video clips are a bit more pricey, though, and probably not a good use of funds for personal projects, but if you're going for the big Hollywood production look (or shooting for an Oscar), they might be a better investment.

Let's Do It!

You don't have to make any decisions just yet about your DVD's aesthetics. Whether you want a motion or still backdrop or whether you want a fancy font for titles are choices that you can make later. Your first task is to figure out in which menu you'll put your movies and slideshows. That's right, your DVD can have more than one menu—many more. Now is the time to decide which of your elements will go in the opening menu and which will go in secondary menus.

You can have up to six buttons in each menu. If you want all of them to go on the opening screen and you have no more than six items, then you're done with your planning.

Personally, even if I had only six items to show off, I'd arrange them in more than one menu. You can go for a more interesting organization that way. And if you have more than six elements, you have no choice but to go the multiple-menu route. Get out your pen and paper or fire up your planning software and make a simple drawing of the structure of your DVD.

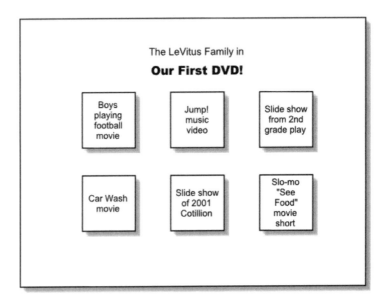

The LeVitus Family in

Our First DVD!

Boys playing football movie	Jump! music video	Slide show from 2nd grade play
Car Wash movie	Slide show of 2001 Cotillion	Slo-mo "See Food" movie short

Of course you don't have to plan this, especially if you only have a few items. But the more assets you have, the more you'll benefit from this up-front investment. It's more effort to rearrange the menus later than to plan them right ahead of time.

For my project, I want one video and two slideshows on the opening menu. That adds up to three items, but I need to include a fourth item in this menu—a button that takes viewers to a secondary menu. That's where I'm going to put two more videos. If I wanted, I could add another button to the second menu to take viewers to yet another menu.

It sounds more complicated than it is. Once you've worked with iDVD a few times and seen how it uses folders to hold the secondary menu's contents it'll become second nature to you.

Import Movies and Images

Now set your plans in front of you and—yes, it's time to actually launch iDVD. Yea! If your sample project comes up on-screen, select New Project from the File menu for a fresh start.

It doesn't matter what theme is showing. Whatever it is, it's just serving as a placeholder while you import your media assets.

Why do you want to start importing assets before you diddle with the theme? Glad you asked! The reason is that iDVD will encode them in the background while you play with themes and buttons, but only if you import them first.

On the other hand, if you're already well-versed in iDVD, you certainly could choose the appropriate theme now. But since we're going to change it soon, don't bother—just use whatever's showing so you can get the encoding process started.

Import movies

If you have any movies on the plan for your opening menu, put them in the menu you have on-screen now. There are a couple of ways to do this.

Drag the movie file from the Finder onto the iDVD screen, as shown in **Figure 5.2**.

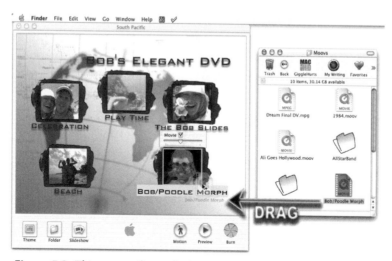

Figure 5.2 This seems the easiest way to import content, at least in my humble opinion.

Or you can go to the File menu, choose Import, then Video, as shown in **Figure 5.3.** Finally, navigate to your movie file and select it.

Figure 5.3 Maybe it's me, but I think this is more work than drag and drop.

Voilà, iDVD places a button in the menu for playing your movie. It's just like the process you followed for the tutorial in Chapter 3, but this time you're using your own material.

If you have the Motion button turned on, your movie should be playing now within the movie button. That much motion can be annoying while you're trying to work, but you can turn it off by clicking the Motion button.

Be sure to save your work frequently, just as you do in your word processor or any program that requires saving changes. It's easy to get wrapped up in all the fun of creating your project and forget this crucial task.

The good news is that when iDVD crashes it doesn't take down the whole Mac with it the way it used to in Mac OS 9. The bad news is that it does sometimes crash, and you still lose everything since the last save.

Import images for slideshows

The process for importing slideshows is different from that for importing movies. You must create a button first and then import images. Just click the Slideshow button below the menu or choose Add Slideshow from the Project menu to make the button appear. Then double-click the new button to open the slideshow editor.

Importing your images is now a simple matter of dragging them from your project folder in the Finder and dropping them into the slideshow editor. You can put up to 99 slides in each slideshow, and you can have up to six slideshows per screen (menu).

While you have the slideshow editor open (see **Figure 5.4**), let's do a little customizing. You can make the thumbnail images of your slides large or small by choosing the size from the Thumbnail pop-up menu.

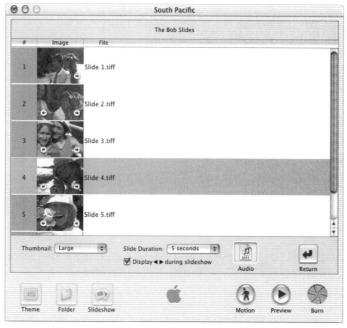

Fig 5.4 You can view your images in two different sizes in the slideshow editor. Enlarge them, as I have here, so that you can see them well. Or keep them small so that you have a better view of the number and order of your slides.

Slideshow vs. slideshow

The distinction between buttons that you create on the iDVD menu and the buttons below it that come with iDVD can be confusing. For instance, there's a Slideshow button (with a capital S) *below* the menu. And there's also a slideshow button (with a little S) *on* the menu. And they're two entirely different objects. How much more confusing does it get than that? The difference is, of course, that you create the one that goes on the menu and the other one is inextricably part of the iDVD application.

How long do you want each image on your slideshow to stay on screen? You can choose 1, 3, 5, or 10 seconds from the Duration pop-up menu. Or you can leave it on the default Manual option to let viewers click through your slides at their own speed. The other option for duration is Fit to Audio. This is a good choice if you're planning to have sound play during the slideshow, since it'll match the speed of the slideshow to the length of the audio clip. (I'll discuss this in greater detail, as well as how to import audio, in Chapter 7.)

It's easy to change the order of your slides. Say that you want slide 2 to come after slide 4. Just drag the slide's image in the slideshow editor to the right spot.

You can add forward and back arrows to your slideshow by checking the "Display during slideshow" box. Viewers won't be able to click the arrows on-screen to advance or reverse your slideshow, but the arrows will indicate which buttons to push on the remote control. Basically, your audience will know if they're at the beginning, middle, or end of your slideshow by looking at the arrows.

Those are all the choices you have to make for now. Click the Return button to go back to the opening menu.

Create More Menus

You can make your DVD's structure as complicated as you like, with as many branches as a willow tree. But don't go crazy or you'll lose your viewers. Simpler is often better.

Making an additional menu is easy. Just click the Folder button under the opening menu and a new button appears on-screen. It's not pretty, but remember, we're saving the dressing up for later. The purpose of this button is to get us to another menu. Double-click the button (or highlight it and press Return) and you'll be magically transported to a new menu that contains nothing more than an arrow button and a generic title. Add slideshows, movies, and other folder buttons—according to your plan—following the same steps you used to add items to the opening menu.

After you've finished adding items to this menu, click the arrow button to return to the previous menu.

Add as many menus full of movies and slideshows as you need to complete the structure of your DVD and let's move on to making it look pretty.

Creating Menus and Buttons

Now that your videos and slideshows are right where you want them, it's time to dress up your project. Take control of the theme, choosing backdrops for menus and shapes for buttons, to let you create the look you want for your movies and slideshows.

With iDVD 2 you have a great deal of control over how your DVD looks, and not just which items appear on what menu. You can choose from among the 14 themes Apple includes with iDVD, such as a background of floating clouds or a still image of parchment paper. Or you can create a custom backdrop from one of your own movies or still images. Maybe you want a dinosaur backdrop for Uncle Yogi's 50th birthday video (all in good-natured fun, of course) or a video of your child's first wobbly steps playing in the background of an entire menu (be careful not to go overboard with motion menus, though—you don't want to make your viewers queasy). Simply start with one of iDVD's built-in themes and modify it to your liking.

Take Control of Menus

There's nothing wrong with going the easy route and using one of the themes Apple supplies with iDVD. They're designed by professionals, so you can't go wrong with any of them.

Then again, why not have a little fun? Go on—experiment with different designs, even if you're design-shy. You can always go back to one of the supplied themes if you don't like what you end up with. But chances are you'll come up with something great that reflects your own personality.

Let's start with menus.

Pick a starting point

Open the project you started in Chapter 5, if it's not already on-screen, and prepare to modify it. Scroll through iDVD's gallery of themes (see **Figure 6.1**) until you find one that has elements you'd like to keep, such as an attractive button shape or a nice title font. Even if you don't want to use every element in the theme, if there are parts you'll want to keep, you're that much further ahead in designing the look of your DVD.

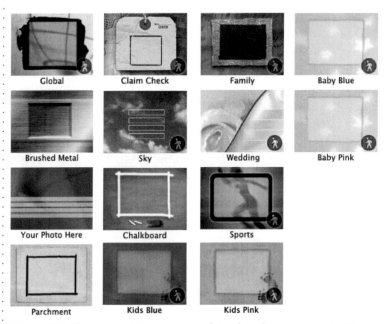

Global   Claim Check   Family   Baby Blue

Brushed Metal   Sky   Wedding   Baby Pink

Your Photo Here   Chalkboard   Sports

Parchment   Kids Blue   Kids Pink

Figure 6.1 If you want to use one of Apple's themes as a starting point or even as your finished look, you have these 14 to choose from.

It's important to choose a theme you can work with before you make any modifications. If you start customizing parts and then decide you want to try out a different theme, all of your changes will be wiped out and you'll have to redesign it all from scratch.

 The 10 themes with the little running person in a circle are motion menus.

The four without the running dude are non-moving themes.

Change the menu title

The next thing to do is change something that's been bugging me ever since we started this project—the generic title, like Sky or Parchment, that comes with each of Apple's themes. Click on the title to highlight it and then type in the real title for your project (see **Figure 6.2**). If you want to change the font, open the Theme panel and click the Customize tab to open the Customize panel. Now choose a font from the Font pop-up menu in the Title area of this panel.

Figure 6.2 I changed the title of my DVD project from "Brushed Metal" to "Oh, Baby," since my project documents the infant stage of a child's life.

You can move the title wherever you want on the menu if you choose Custom from the Position pop-up menu in that same Title area. That unlocks its position, then you can drag it around with your cursor. If you prefer not to have a title at all, choose No Title from the Position pop-up menu.

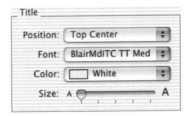

Customize the background image

Now let's get the right image into the background. Unless you want to keep the one that's already there, find the custom image that you want to fill up the opening menu's backdrop. Drag that image's file from your desktop (or your project folder, if you've organized your assets there) onto the menu in iDVD or into the Image/Movie well in the Background area of the Customize panel.

You can also do this by selecting Import > Image from the File menu.

If you want to use a video for the background instead, drag the video file into the Image/Movie well or select Import > Background Movie from the File menu. It won't work to drag the file onto iDVD's menu; all that does is add another button to the menu. Don't forget about the lovely undersea video that comes with Apple's tutorial. If you want to use that for your background, go get it from the Media folder inside the Tutorial folder.

Maybe the image or movie you've chosen doesn't look as good as you thought it would. It's easy enough to get rid of it. Either import a new image or movie and it will be automatically replaced or drag it out of the Image/Movie well. It'll disappear in a puff of smoke.

There's just one other bit of cleanup we need to do before we move on to having fun with buttons—you may want to expunge that Apple logo watermark hanging out so visibly in the lower-right corner of your DVD menu. Although you didn't have the option of getting rid of it in iDVD 1, now you can with version 2. Select Preferences from the iDVD menu and uncheck Show Watermark.

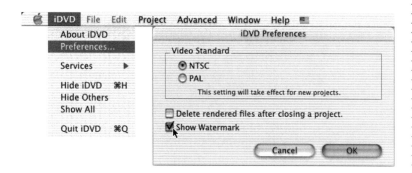

Have Your Way with Buttons

You have even more flexibility in designing your buttons than you do with your menus. You can move them, pick new shapes, and use still or moving images for the actual button. And there's one extra trick: You can choose one frame from a movie as a button image.

To move buttons where you want on the menu, first free them up from their locked position—choose Free Position from the Button area of the Customize panel. Then drag them as you please. To make sure that the buttons (and the title, for that matter) don't drop off the edge of the screen for viewers watching your DVD on a television, select Show TV Safe Area from the Advanced menu or use the keyboard shortcut Command-T. iDVD will help you out by drawing a box on your menu to show you where to confine your elements, as shown in **Figure 6.3.**

Figure 6.3 Keep your arms and legs in, ladies and gentlemen. And keep your buttons and titles within the TV safe area.

To change the shape of buttons, choose from among the shapes in the shape pop-up menu in the Button area of the Customize panel.

For heaven's sake, change the titles of your buttons to something more meaningful than Slideshow or the file name of your movies—click the button title and type. You can also move the button titles to sit under, above, to the side, or right on top of their buttons by choosing the position you want from the Position pop-up menu in the Button area of the Customize panel. Change the font if you like also, but beware of the same problem that plagued desktop publishing when the power came to the people. Different fonts for buttons and menu titles could clash.

One more option with fonts is to increase or decrease their size using the Size slider in the Button area.

As part of your efforts to save your hard work as you go, if you've come up with an overall design you may want to use again, save it as a Favorite (click the Save in Favorites button at the bottom of the Customize panel). When you do, iDVD will add it to the theme choices.

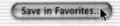

To share your fantastic new theme with everyone who uses your computer, click the "Shared for all users" check box when you name your new favorite.

Select Favorites in the Themes pop-up menu to find a favorite quickly.

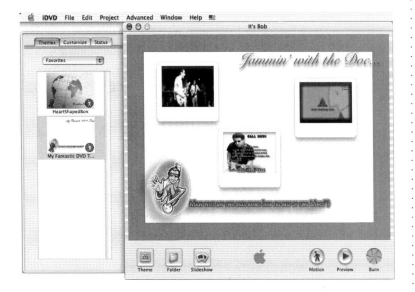

It's not quite that easy to remove a favorite from the Theme panel. You can't do it from within iDVD. Instead, you have to quit iDVD, locate the Favorites folder in the Finder (in your Home folder under Library/iDVD/Favorites). Then drag the favorite you want to delete to the Trash. One proviso: If you checked the "Shared for all users" check box you'll instead find it in the Library folder at the root level of the disk under iDVD/Favorites. (See Figure 6.4.)

Figure 6.4 The only hard part about getting rid of a favorite theme is finding it: Your own themes are in your Home folder Library, but shared themes are in the root-level Library.

Probably the most fun part about fiddling with buttons is deciding what image to use. As I said, you have even more options than with the background for menus.

The simplest is to use a still image. Just drag an image file to the button on the iDVD menu. For slideshow buttons, you can also choose any of the slides in the show as the button image. Click on the button to select it and then move the slider above the button until you find the image you want.

You can apply a moving image by dragging a movie file on top of a button. The other cool trick is to use one of the frames of your movie as the image for a button. To do that, drag a movie file onto the button and click the button to highlight it and make a slider appear above it. Uncheck the Movie option above the slider, then move the slider until you find the frame you want, as shown in **Figure 6.5.** Click anywhere on the menu to get rid of the slider. This technique only works for movie buttons, not slideshow buttons.

Figure 6.5 Using frames from your movies increases your options for custom button images; choose a frame by moving the slider above the movie button.

To add a little variety you can also change the duration of a movie that's playing on a motion button. One way to do this is to move the Motion Duration slider in the Customize panel. But that will affect the length of clips playing on the menu as well.

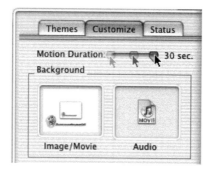

So, here's a different technique to try instead: Play just a few frames of a video on a movie button over and over by selecting the button and dragging the slider to near the end. Make sure the Movie option is checked. Turn on Motion (click the button or use the shortcut Command-J) and you'll see a very short clip that plays over and over quickly on this button. Depending on your footage it may look like a short slideshow that toggles between one or two images.

If you need to remove a button, just click it and press Delete on your keyboard. Buttons can also be copied, pasted, and deleted the same way you copy, paste, and delete text in a word processor.

Now step back and have a look at your entire project. The only thing that's missing are sound clips, but you can examine the look of your project by clicking the Preview button. Be sure to turn on motion with the Motion button before you do. If you're satisfied with what you see, it's time to move on to the next step: adding sound to slideshows and menus.

Adding Audio

The finishing touch is to add sound to your DVD. You already have sound playing with movies if you included sound in the original movie file. But you can also add sound that will play while viewers flip through the images of your slideshows and sound that plays while viewers are considering which menu button to click next. In other words, we're going to talk about the background music that plays when a menu is on-screen.

Getting sound into iDVD is the simple part. But preparing it takes a little more thought and action. There are many different sources for sound—CDs, clips that Apple supplies, or your own recordings. Preparing each one requires slightly different steps, so I'll lay those out for you first, then tell you the easy part—how to get them into iDVD.

Once you're done adding sound to your DVD, all that's left to do is preview and burn it.

Gather Your Sound Clips

Just as there are many sources for finding images, there are probably even more for free sound clips, starting with the umpteen files that Apple gives you with iDisk. It's a great resource that can add a lot to your production, and the best part is that it's totally free.

You access these files through your iDisk. If you don't already have iDisk in a toolbar, select Customize Toolbar from the Finder's View menu. Up pops a folder full of icons with an iDisk icon among them. Drag the iDisk icon into the toolbar at the top of the open folder and click Done. Then click the icon in the toolbar, open the Software folder, then the Extras folder, and finally the FreePlay Music folder.

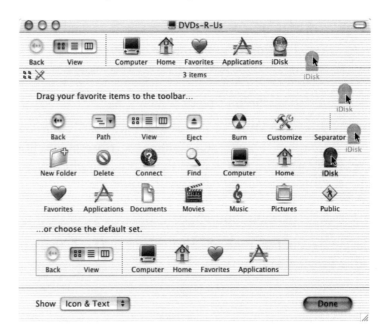

First, you'll need to make sure that your computer is set up for Internet access. Visit the Network pane in System Preferences and enter the settings supplied by your Internet service provider. Then go to the Internet preference pane and enter your iDisk account information.

Now you should see many sound clips that are yours for the taking, as shown in **Figure 7.1.**

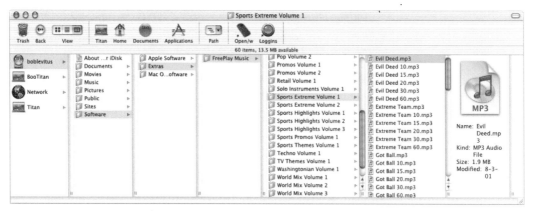

Figure 7.1 You'll have more files than you know what to do with after opening up the FreePlay Music folder in your iDisk.

Drag the sound files you'd like to sample onto your hard drive. If you try to play them from within the FreePlay Music folder it won't work as well, since you'll be listening to them stream over the Internet. Once they're on your hard drive, double-click one at a time to listen to them.

If you choose the Column view in the Finder you can play them by clicking the Play Sound button in the preview pane, like this:

It's a good idea to put the ones that you want to use for your project with your other assets inside your iDVD project folder, just to stay organized.

If you want to access the FreePlay Music folder frequently, make an alias and put it on your desktop or in your Dock. When you open it, you'll go directly to the FreePlay Music folder. This shortcut saves a lot of time because you don't have to navigate through several folders, each of which takes a couple minutes to open.

Apple also supplies you one sample audio clip with iDVD. It's called Slideshow audio.mp3 and is in the Media folder (inside the iTunes Tutorial folder). It's a snappy little Latin number that's sure to make your DVD viewers want to dance.

Another source of free music is your own audio CDs. Beware the long arm of the law, though; chances are you're borrowing copyrighted materials if you're taking songs from a CD. Be sure to get permission or a license to use the songs if you're making the DVD for commercial purposes. That precaution noted, here's how you can grab music from a CD to use on your DVD.

Although you can import audio directly into iDVD from a CD (choose Import > Audio from the File menu), this doesn't do you any good, because iDVD doesn't do the actual importing until you click the Burn button. But then you can't put a blank DVD-R in the SuperDrive, because the program won't let you eject the audio CD, which is the source of some of the files it needs to burn the disk. It's a classic catch-22.... Therefore, you must extract the audio from the CD before you import it into iDVD. The easiest way to do this is with iTunes.

To extract a track with iTunes, launch iTunes and insert an audio CD. iTunes may connect to the Web to look for title information (you can tell it not to in Preferences). If the CD icon isn't highlighted in the Source list, click it. A list of the tracks on the CD will appear to the right. Click the check box for any you want to import and then click the Import button in the upper-right corner of the iTunes window.

Be careful...iTunes' default is to import all the songs on the disc. So make sure only the song or songs you desire have their check boxes checked.

iTunes will now extract the track from the CD, create a sound file, and place that sound file on your hard drive in the iTunes folder inside the Documents folder. This folder is in your Users folder.

iTunes will import the file in whichever format you've set in the Import tab of the Preference window. By default it will import the file as an MP3. You can change this to AIFF or WAV. If you want the best sound possible, change the setting to AIFF. The trade off is that AIFF files are 10 times bigger than MP3 files.

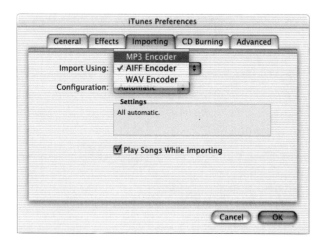

OK, now that you have the sound file on your Mac's hard drive (again, I'd recommend transferring it into your iDVD project folder), you can import it into iDVD, along with any other sound files on your hard drive.

Import Sound

There are two different ways you can use sound in your DVD, either playing in the background of a menu or in the background of a slideshow.

Musical menu background

It's nice for viewers to have music to listen to while they decide which of your slideshows and videos to look at. So why not add some ambiance to your opening menu? Here's how:

1. Open the menu and click the Theme button to open up the Theme panel.

2. Click Customize, then drag the sound file from your hard drive into the Audio well near the top of the Customize panel.

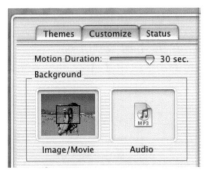

Don't forget—iDVD will only play the first 30 seconds of the music (or whatever value you set the Motion Duration slider to).

If you don't hear the sound, that probably means you don't have motion turned on. Just click the Motion button (or press Command-J) to get the sound effect.

Musical slideshow background

And why not have a little music to accompany your slide-shows? Let your viewers dance to a little samba music while they watch or soothe them with something symphonic. No matter what your choice, all you need do to add accompaniment to a slideshow is double-click the slideshow's button on the iDVD menu. That opens up the slideshow editor. Now drag the audio file into the Audio well in the lower-right portion of the editor, as shown in **Figure 7.2.**

Figure 7.2 It's a one-two process to get sound to play with a slideshow. Open the slideshow editor and drag the file into the Audio well.

But wait. You have an important decision to make. Unless you want your sound to get cut off prematurely or restart several times, you ought to fiddle with the Slide Duration pop-up menu. You already set the timing before if you were following along in Chapter 5, but now that you know exactly what sound clip you're using, you may need to adjust the duration again.

Fit To Audio is my favorite choice because it makes your slideshow last exactly as long as the audio clip. So there won't be any awkward breaks or stops. (iDVD does have its limits, thank goodness—the minimum slide duration is 1 second.) But if your audio clip is short and you have a lot of slides to show, that's not such a good choice. In that case, it's better to let the sound loop and choose Manual or 1, 3, 5, or 10 seconds from the pop-up menu. If you choose Manual, the sound will loop until the end of the slideshow and then stop abruptly. Not the most elegant, but that's your only option if you want to use sound and also let viewers control the speed of the slideshow.

Add sound to each slideshow and menu that you want to have it, and—you're not going to believe this—you're just about finished. Congratulations. You've completed all but one last step: You should still preview your entire project before you burn it, to make sure there are no glitches (make sure motion is on, then press the Preview button).

Refer back to Chapter 3 if you need a quick reminder of how to burn your project to disc.

part 3

Wrapping Up

How to Back Up or Archive iDVD Projects

You may have noticed by now that the contents of even the smallest DVD project consume a massive amount of disk space. For example, the smallest DVD project I've done so far contained just 9 or 10 minutes of video, yet it used just over half a gigabyte of disk space. And that was only what ended up being used in the final DVD. If you count all the raw footage I imported, all the interim versions of movies I saved, all the versions of all the still pictures and sounds (both used and rejected), and everything else used in the production, we're talking about closer to 2 GB.

As you might imagine, a DVD with more content—say 60 or 90 minutes of video—might well use more than 4 GB of disk space. With raw footage, interim versions, graphics, audio, and any other content, a single DVD project can easily require more than 20 GB of disk space before you're through with it.

I don't know about you, but I don't have room on my hard disk for more than one or two 20 GB iDVD project folders at a time. So when I complete a project, I usually back it up (twice or three times if it's particularly important to me), then delete the original from my hard disk. If I've put a lot of work into a movie or DVD project, I'll back it up regularly *during* the production process, too.

You don't *have* to back up your iDVD or iMovie projects, but you might *want* to. In this chapter I'll show you various ways to back up or archive mass quantities of data, along with tips, hints, and advice on hardware and software that makes the whole affair nearly painless.

Backup Considerations

Before we consider the types of hardware and software you might use to back up your projects, let's step back for a second and look at the big picture.

We'll start with a list of some things to think about before you decide what (if any) hardware or software you might need.

- Could the source material be easily replaced? If not, those files ought to be backed up.

- How much data is going to be backed up?

- How often will you back up?

- How many disks, tapes, or cartridges will it require?

- How much will that media cost?

- How long will a full backup take? An incremental backup?

- Do you want to automate the process so it occurs whether you remember or not?

Once you've given some thought to these questions you can start answering more specific ones, like which files need to be backed up, what hardware is most appropriate and cost-effective for your needs, and what software, if any, you should use to back up your project files.

What to Back Up

First of all, whenever you think about backing up, start by considering what impact losing everything on your hard disk would have on your life. If that wouldn't bother you, don't bother backing up anything.

> *But mark my words: There will come a day when you'll regret not backing up at least some files. Surely there's at least one file on that disk that would be missed.*

Only you can decide if the source files associated with your project are important enough to back up. Imagine for a moment that your hard drive has vaporized and is gone forever.

> *Don't laugh—it happens more often than you think.*

Did your iMovies take a long time to edit and render? If so, back them up. Or, if you still have the original footage on DV tape, consider whether it would it be easier (or cheaper) to re-import and re-edit the movie or movies.

Which brings us to our first specific consideration: Do you need to back up all or some of your source material? And, if so, how often should you do it?

> *Source material refers to the original movies, still graphics, sound, and other content files used in your DVD.*

In addition to backing up the source files, you need to consider how much time you've invested in the iDVD project itself. If you had to, could you re-create the entire DVD from scratch? And, more importantly, would you want to?

> *Also consider how long it will take to re-create the source material, if you don't back it up as well.*

If you have much time invested and don't want to redo it all, back up the iDVD project file as well as the source material files.

> *The project file is the one with the dvdproj suffix (usually) and an icon like this:*

The Dr. Mac
Attack.dvdproj

What to Back Up To

What are you going to do to back up those files? You need to copy them from your hard disk to some other type of medium. There are more hardware options than I could possibly do justice to in this space, but a handful stand out, including one or two you won't have to spend any more money on.

Use the hardware Apple gave you—your SuperDrive

You already own at least one suitable device—your SuperDrive. A SuperDrive makes an excellent backup device, but the cost of media may be prohibitive.

Don't forget you can burn CD-R/RW as well as DVD-R discs in a SuperDrive.

The biggest issue is whether a SuperDrive will be cost effective. DVD-R discs are relatively expensive and can only be used once; CD-R and CD-RW discs are inexpensive, but only hold 700 MB or less each. If your project and source materials are large, backing up may require dozens of discs, which means you'll have to baby-sit the process and spend a lot of time feeding discs to your SuperDrive.

You can also, at least in theory, use 4.7 GB DVD-RW discs, which can be erased and reused. But Apple doesn't recommend DVD-RW discs and neither Retrospect (backup software; see next section) nor iDVD currently supports them. I've had mixed results using DVD-RW discs with Roxio Toast Titanium, though the latest version at this writing (5.1.3) seems to work most of the time.

The nice thing about DVD-RW discs is that you can erase and reuse them again and again, and they're not much more expensive than blank DVD-R discs. Being your humble servant, I ran out to Fry's and CompUSA just now and bought DVD-R and DVD-RW blank discs. DVD-R discs from Apple were $25 for five, or $5 each.

Here's a first—the Apple-branded DVD-R discs, which are recommended by Apple and are certified to burn at 2X with iDVD, were the least expensive.

Sony and Pioneer DVD-RW discs were $15 each; TDK and Verbatim discs were $9.99.

Or use your camcorder

The other suitable device you may already own is a camcorder, which is a great way to back up movies. You use iMovie to export them to inexpensive DV tape in real time, so backing up an hour of movies will take an hour—no more and no less— and only cost a few bucks for a DV tape.

Here's how: Choose Export Movie from the File menu, then choose To Camera in the Export pop-up menu and click Export. The movie will be exported to the tape in your camcorder.

Then, if you ever need the movie again it will only take a few moments to re-import from camcorder to Mac using FireWire. This is often the most cost-effective way to reduce your need for expensive backup media such as DVD-R discs.

Speaking of inexpensive DV tapes, you might want to consider not erasing or reusing any of your source tapes, especially any with material that's worth saving. Then, in a worst-case scenario, you could re-edit from these original source tapes, which is often better than losing footage forever.

Other hardware solutions

Of course, you can use almost any kind of storage device for backups—CD-R/RW, Zip, Jaz, optical disk, or tape. Or you might decide it's easier to back everything up to another hard disk. If you have fast Internet access, you can even back up files to a remote disk or to your Apple iDisk.

One last device to consider if you back up a lot of data is a tape drive. The advantage of a tape drive is that the medium is inexpensive (per megabyte), transfer speeds are impressive, and the tapes hold massive quantities of data.

At the top of the tape-drive food chain are DLT (digital linear tape) drives, which offer speeds up to 11 MB per second and as much as 220 GB of storage per tape. They're impressive looking beasts, as you can see in **Figure 8.1**.

Think about how many unattended backups you could do with a 220 GB tape!

Figure 8.1
LaCie (www.lacie.com)
DLT drives cost $1,500 to
$4,000 depending upon
capacity and features; tapes
come in sizes from 40 GB
to 220 GB (the largest ones
available today) and cost
$75 to $150.

*There's actually another reason to consider DLT if you're
serious about your DVD authoring. Commercial (store-
bought) discs, as well as some discs created with high-end
DVD authoring software (such as Apple's DVD Studio Pro),
can make discs that contain up to 9 GB, or over 2 hours, of
video. These higher-capacity discs are called "DVD-9," but
a SuperDrive can't make them. You first need to author the
DVD then export it to DLT, which a commercial DVD dupli-
cator can use as a DVD-9 master.*

Optical vs. Magnetic Storage

Remember, no matter what kind of magnetic medium you use, whether
it's in your camcorder or a high-falutin' DLT drive or a disk like a Zip
or a Jaz or a FireWire hard drive, your data will always be less safe
than if it's backed up to some kind of optical medium.

Why? Simple: The substrate of tape (the plastic tape itself) has a
relatively short lifespan of only a few years. Also, anything recorded
magnetically is subject to the vicissitudes of the Earth's magnetic field
and those of other magnetic devices, which can screw up the intricately
aligned patterns of iron particles embedded in the tape or disk. Plus,
tape is somewhat fragile, and can easily become tangled, creased,
or otherwise damaged.

In an optical medium (such as CD and DVD), your data is frozen into
the actual physical structure of the material on the disk, and it can't
be perturbed by anything as feeble as a household (or terrestrial)
magnetic field. And it's encased in some pretty tough plastic, so it's
well protected from environmental shocks.

Burning data onto DVD-R disks with the SuperDrive will protect it for
a long time; backing up to tape will protect your data, but perhaps
not as well or for as long. Caveat emptor.

What to Back Up With

Do you need specialized backup software to back up your movies or iDVD projects? Absolutely not. All you need to do is keep all the files associated with the project in a single folder, then burn that folder onto a CD-R/RW or DVD-R as often as you like.

Or a DVD-RW, with the aforementioned proviso.

I would like to add, though, that while you don't need any software whatsoever to back up a few movies or an iDVD project, you might want a backup or synchronization program anyway.

Just because you don't really need it for video/DVD backups, that doesn't mean you don't need really need it. Not only will such software allow you to automate and simplify your video and DVD backups, you can use it for all your important documents (and anything else you choose to back up), and just include the video and DVD folders you want to back up in your everyday backup routine.

There are dozens of Mac OS X–savvy programs to choose from. One inexpensive shareware program is the elegant $20 Chrono-Sync from Econ Technologies (www.econtechnologies.com).

I like this little company. Its motto is "The customer is our consultant" and it stands by that. ChronoSync has been updated with bug fixes and feature improvements three times in as many months.

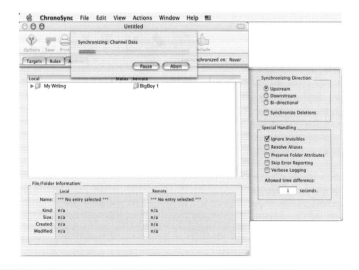

Then there's the inexpensive ($49) non-shareware program Retrospect Express, from Dantz Development:

A Word About Backing Up in General

Begin rant:

You *are* backing up your important files every day, aren't you? If you aren't, read this sidebar carefully—it could save your bacon.

If your computer and all the files on it were to vaporize tomorrow, how badly would you be hurt? If your answer was anything but "not a bit," you should have a backup plan in place and adhere to it religiously.

Speaking of which, any file important enough to back up is important enough to back up three times, with one backup always stored in another location. That way, even if your Mac and everything in the same room were destroyed or stolen, you'd be able to restore all but your most recent work from the off-site backup. If that's overkill, even two sets, with one stored off-site, is better than having your only backup go up in flames along with your Mac.

One last thing: Doing it right may not be cheap. You need blank media (discs, disks, tapes, or whatever), and you may need additional hardware and software, not to mention time spent on setup and execution.

Before you have a cow, consider the alternative. DriveSavers is a professional data recovery firm, complete with clean room and bunny suits. Though their clients (including Sting, Clarence Clemmons, Sean Connery, Keith Richards, and Industrial Light and Magic) sing their praises, they charge accordingly—founder Scott Gaidano has a gorgeous Ferarri. And even DriveSavers can't recover every file from every disk every time. Sometimes even they strike out (but you still pay).

There are only two kinds of Mac users: Those who *have* lost data and those who *will*. Don't wait until you're a loser to get with the program The only *real* protection for your files is multiple backups—just do it.

End rant.

Zulch, the God of Data Security

I recommend Retrospect backup software from Dantz Development (www.dantz.com). Period. There are several versions available, from Express ($49) for personal backups to Server ($799) for multiple mixed network backups.

I've used Retrospect backup products for at least 10 years and have never lost a bit (or a byte, for that matter) of data. I've tried many other backup and synchronization programs, and most of them don't stink. But when it comes to my data, I'm more comfortable entrusting it to the experienced engineers at Dantz. I use the Retrospect Desktop product ($150), but the less-expensive Retrospect Express only lacks one or two of its features (such as extensive file-level filtering and tape drive support). By the way, all of the different versions of Retrospect look exactly like the picture to the left.

Founded by brothers Larry and Richard Zulch, Dantz Development has been making Mac backup solutions since the Mac debuted, way back in 1984. I suppose another reason I trust Retrospect so much is that I know where to find the Zulch brothers if need be. Fortunately, in all these years I've never had to.

I tend to be quite paranoid about losing files, so my backup plan is designed to allow me to get back to "the way things were" as quickly as possible after a crash or other unnatural disaster. Since I hate the thought of re-creating even a single file, I have three complete backups of my entire Documents folder burned onto DVD-R discs—one set is in my safe deposit box, one set is in the trunk of my car, and the third set is here in my office. At the end of each week I swap the office set for one of the off-site sets so I'll never lose more than a few days of work in the very worst case.

And it would have to be a pretty bad case, indeed, because in addition to my three DVD backup sets, I also back up my Documents folder to an external FireWire hard disk every day. Then I back it up again to a second FireWire hard disk. Every day. Finally, I back up my Home folder, iDVD (or iMovie) project folders, and other vital folders three times a day on top of my daily regimen.

Better still, all of my backups to hard disks occur automatically and in the background, whether I'm at the keyboard or not, and without a bit of human intervention. If that appeals to you, reread the section earlier in this chapter about Retrospect, which is what I depend upon to accomplish this feat.

My method may be overkill, but I sleep well at night knowing that no matter what happens, I can be back in business within a few hours.

One last thing: Be sure you test your backup solution before a problem occurs. Make sure it does just what you expect when you restore from it.

iDVD in Depth

This chapter is unlike any other. We're going out with a bang—a brief but comprehensive reference for every menu item, button, panel, window, and pane in iDVD.

In many cases, I will point you to another chapter for additional information. Even when I do, this chapter briefly describes the feature, what it does, and how to use it.

So when you're trying to figure out how a particular iDVD feature works, refer to this chapter first. Think of it as a big, friendly cheat-sheet.

We'll start with every item in every menu, then look at all the buttons, and finally, delve into the Theme drawer.

The Menus

The menus—iDVD, File, Edit, Project, Advanced, Window, and Help—are where much of the action in iDVD begins and ends. If you know what each menu contains and what each item does, working with iDVD will be faster and easier.

Most of the menu items have keyboard shortcuts. Learn them and use them. They're faster than reaching for the menu.

That said, let's look at those menus one by one, from left to right, starting with...

The iDVD menu

There's really only one item of much interest in the iDVD menu: the **Preferences** item, shown in **Figure 9.1**.

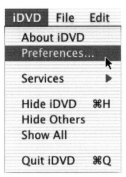

Figure 9.1 Preferences is the only item of real interest here.

In every Mac program, an ellipsis at the end of a menu item indicates that selecting the item won't have any immediate effect. Instead, choosing the item opens a window with additional choices and options, as shown in **Figure 9.2**.

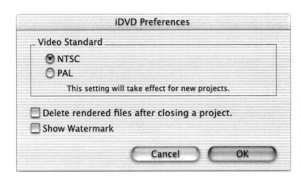

Figure 9.2 The iDVD Preferences window has three options.

In the Video Standard section, choose NTSC or PAL depending on what the standard is in your country. It's NTSC here in the United States and PAL in most of Europe and Asia.

If you're not sure, check the manual for your camcorder, VCR, or television set. One of them should say NTSC or PAL somewhere.

The check box for "Delete rendered files after closing a project" requires a bit of explaining. Its purpose is to help you conserve space on your hard disk. Here's why that's important:

When it comes time to burn your DVD to disc you'll need a certain amount of free space on your hard disk or the burn will fail. The rule of thumb is that you need at least half as much free space on your disk as there is DV content on your DVD. So if your DVD contains 12 GB of original DV movie files (roughly 1 hour), you should try to keep at least 6 GB free.

If you select the check box, when you quit or close the project iDVD will automatically delete only the MPEG files it rendered in the background. Your original DV movie files are untouched. The only downside is that iDVD will have to re-encode the movie files again before you can burn the project, which could take several hours.

Oh, I know what you're thinking. Why let iDVD delete them at all? Why not just do it yourself if space gets tight on your hard disk? What's so hard about dragging a file to the Trash and emptying it?

Here's where it gets tricky. OS X and iDVD hide those render files from you. If you want to delete the files manually, you'll have a hard time finding them unless you know the secret, which, of course, I'm about to share with you. Here it is: Your project document isn't really a document. It may look like a document, but it's really an OS X container known as a *package*. In this case, it's a package masquerading as a document, but packages may also pretend to be applications. Many of the icons you think of as applications are actually packages. How can you tell which icons are packages? Read on.

A package is nothing more than a special folder that does one thing when you open it and does something else when you Control-click it and then choose Show Package Contents from the contextual menu, shown in **Figure 9.3.**

Figure 9.3 Ah ha! So that's how you get to the stuff inside a package icon.

When the package opens, open the folder called Contents.

From here on, you can just double-click folders to open them; once the contents of a package are shown it behaves like a regular folder until you close the Contents folder again.

Open the Resources folder inside the Contents folder, then open the MPEG folder in the Resources folder. The files in the MPEG folder are your render files, as shown in **Figure 9.4.** You can now delete them in the usual way if you want to, by dragging them to the Trash.

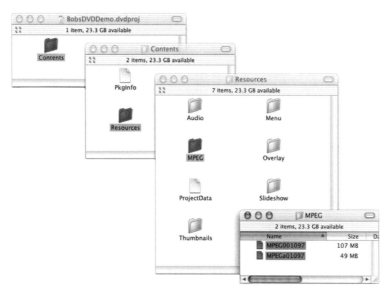

Figure 9.4 MPEG001097 and MPEGa01097 are the rendered versions of two movies in my project, which iDVD would delete for me if I checked the box.

Last but not least, the Show Watermark check box shows and hides the Apple logo. Select the box if you want a semi-transparent Apple logo in the lower-right corner of your DVD, like this:

If you don't want an Apple logo, don't check the box.

The items below Preferences in the iDVD menu—the **Services** submenu, and the **Hide** and **Show** triplets—do the same thing they do in all OS X programs and have no special functions here in iDVD.

Finally, the **Quit** item (shortcut: Command-Q) quits iDVD. But first, it will ask if you want to Save (if you've made changes since your last Save).

The File menu

The File menu (shown in **Figure 9.5**) mostly handles your inter-actions with the items on your hard disk. The File menu's items let you create new projects, open and save existing projects, rename projects (Save As), and import media.

Figure 9.5 The File menu deals primarily with, well, files.

OK then, from the top we have: **New Project** (Command-N), **Open Project** (Command-O), and the **Open Recent** submenu.

New Project begins a new project document (package) with the default name My Great DVD.

If you already have a project open, iDVD politely asks if you'd like to save that project first. That's because iDVD is one of those programs that limits you to opening just one project at a time.

But before iDVD lets you use your new project document, you first have to give it a name and save it to a disk using a Save dialog that looks either like this:

Or like this:

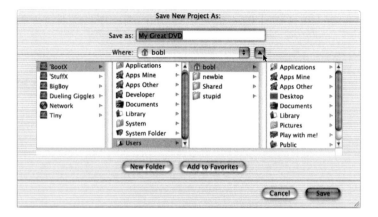

If the Save dialog comes up one way and you'd prefer it the other way, click the triangle where you see the cursor in both of these pictures.

Name your project and click the Save button. A new, empty project window appears with the default Global theme applied.

Open Project serves up a standard Open file dialog box, as shown in **Figure 9.6.**

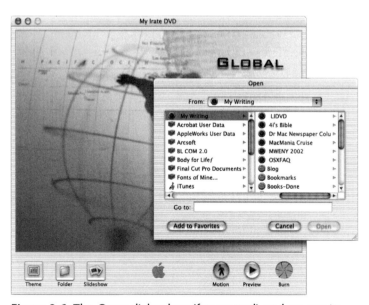

Figure 9.6 The Open dialog box (foreground) and an empty project (background).

Open Recent is a submenu:

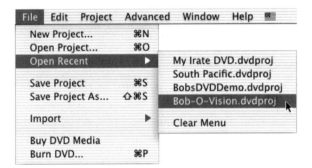

It lets you open any of the last 10 projects you've used directly, without the hassle of navigating an Open file dialog box.

Save Project and **Save Project As** are the usual Mac OS X Save and Save As commands, just like you've seen and used in almost every Mac OS X program ever made.

Import is a submenu:

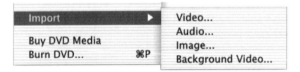

But since Chapter 5 covers that particular function—getting your content into iDVD—we'll leave it at that for now.

Buy DVD Media launches your Web browser and takes you to a page of the Apple Web store where you can buy blank DVD-R discs.

This is one occasion where there may be a reason to buy it from Apple. Apple DVD-R discs are certified to burn at double-speed when used with iDVD 2; many other brands aren't. Furthermore, Apple's price has consistently been as low as or lower than almost anyone else's.

Finally, **Burn DVD** (Command-P) burns the project on a blank DVD-R disc. If you have motion menus in your project and they're turned off, you'll receive a warning first.

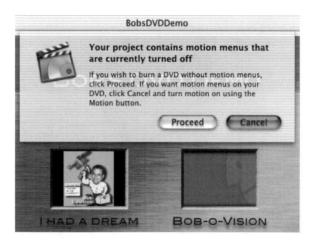

Then it's show time.

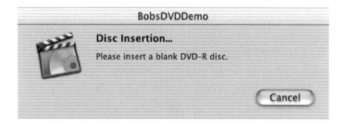

Apparently the Apple Department of Redundancy Department specified it this way. As far as I can tell this menu item and the Burn button and Command-P all do the exact same thing.

The Edit menu

There's nothing unique about this Edit menu—it does the same things it always has in almost every Macintosh program since time immemorial. They say a picture is worth a thousand words, so here's a picture:

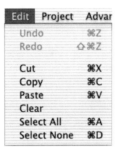

That picture's not gratuitous, either. The one thing about this menu worth noting is the keyboard shortcuts. They're faster and easier than using the menu and they're worth remembering.

One last thing while we're talking about the Edit menu: iDVD offers multiple Undos. That means you can not only Undo the last thing you did in iDVD, but you can also Undo the thing before it, and the thing before that and so on. Usually. And if after undoing all those things you change your mind, you can just Redo them—one, a few, or all. Usually.

Why do I keep saying, "usually"? Because I'm not sure exactly how many steps iDVD remembers, and I'm not sure what makes it forget them. So even though it usually lets you Undo and Redo several steps, the safest bet is to remember to Undo immediately after making a mistake, before doing anything else or saving the project. If you do that, it will work every time.

Even blindfolded in the dark with my hands tied behind my back, my fingers know that Command-Z will Undo and Command-Shift-Z will Redo. These are such great commands that you should memorize their shortcuts even if you memorize no others. They're the key to creative freedom. When you use them, you don't have to worry about making a change and totally screwing up your project. Just Undo it.

If Undo can't save your bacon for whatever reason, there is one last thing you might try: Close the project by clicking the little red gumdrop. (It used to be known as the "Close Box," but that was before it was red and gumdrop-shaped.) If you've made changes since the last time you saved, iDVD will ask if you'd like to save your changes. You don't. So click Don't Save and your project will close without saving. You may lose some changes you wanted to keep but you'll also be rid of the changes that screwed things up.

The Project menu

The Project menu is where commands pertaining to your project live.

Project	Advanced	Window
Project Info...	⌘I
Show Theme Panel	⇧⌘B
Add Folder	⌘K
Add Slideshow	⌘L
Go Back	⌘B

The first item, **Project Info** (Command-I), opens a window that displays each media item—audio, video, or picture—contained in the project, as shown in **Figure 9.7.**

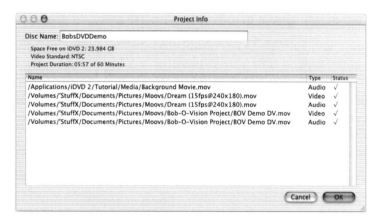

Figure 9.7 This project has five media items in it.

The path to the item is displayed as its name. So the first item is a QuickTime audio file named Background Movie.mov. It's in the Applications folder on my boot disk, in the Media folder, in the Tutorial folder, in the iDVD 2 folder. In Project Info window shorthand, that's Applications/iDVD 2/Tutorial/Media/ Background Movie.mov.

That's all this window does—tell you where your media files reside on your hard disk. Nothing happens if you click, right-click, Control-click, or double-click the items in this list

The next item, **Show/Hide Theme Panel** (Command-Shift-B), is a toggle. Choose it once and it shows the Theme panel; choose it again and it hides the Theme panel. Since *using* the Theme panel is discussed in great detail in Chapter 6, and the items in the Theme panel are described later in this chapter, we'll leave it at that for now.

Add Folder (Command-K) adds a new folder to the current screen.

You can only have six items (folders, slideshows, or movies) on each screen (menu) of your DVD. If you try to add a seventh item, iDVD will gently scold you as shown in **Figure 9.8.**

If you want your DVD to contain more than six items, one of the items on the first screen must be a folder. The folder can contain up to six additional items. But if you need more than 12 total, you have to make one of the items on the second screen a folder. That folder can contain up to six additional items. And so on.

Figure 9.8 No, no, no. You may not do that!

As far as I can determine, there is no limit to the number of folders and subfolders iDVD will let you create. I try to keep my projects as simple as possible, though. The more folders and subfolders you throw into the equation, the more confusing the DVD's navigation.

See Chapter 6 for more about using folders and creating DVD menus.

Add Slideshow (Command-L) adds a new slideshow to the current screen.

See Chapter 6 for more about making slideshows.

The Advanced menu

There's nothing particularly advanced about any of the items in this menu, but I suppose they're more advanced than Cut and Copy. Maybe.

First up is **Show/Hide TV Safe Area** (Command-T). This important item highlights the area of your project that is "title safe." Since most consumer television sets are incapable of displaying a broadcast signal or videotape or DVD image from edge to edge, corner to corner, some part of it always gets cropped. I doubt you want to burn a disk that looks like this:

So you should turn on the TV safe area, which looks like this:

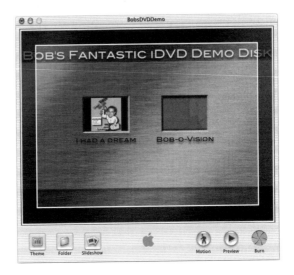

At the very least, use the TV safe area one time just before you burn a DVD. Assume that anything outside the line isn't going to be seen by most (or all) people.

I just leave it on all the time. And I never burn DVDs whose titles spill into the twilight zone outside the TV safe area.

I suggest you just leave it showing all the time. It couldn't hurt and it just might save you $5 some day.

Motion (Command-J), toggles your project's motion menus (if it has them) on or off. Thanks to the Redundancy group, this is the same thing as clicking the Motion button.

> *And, in fact, if you use the menu or keyboard shortcut to turn the motion menus on or off the button emits its soft green glow anyway, just as it would if you'd clicked it.*

Since it's annoying to work in iDVD with motion menus chugging away, and since, as you've seen, iDVD will warn you if you try to burn a DVD with them turned off, you'll probably prefer them off until just before you either Preview or Burn.

> *I frequently leave them off for previewing. Once I've seen them, I don't need to see them every time I preview. But I always check all motion menus and buttons carefully before I burn a DVD, if only to confirm that the poster frame and motion duration I've selected appeal to my eye.*

The last two "Advanced" items—**Apply Theme to Project** and **Apply Theme to Folders**—do pretty much what you'd expect them to. When you select a theme in the Theme panel, it applies to the current screen only. If you want *every screen* in the project to use this theme, choose Apply Theme to Project; if you want every *folder* in the project (but none of your *non-folder* screens) to use this theme, choose Apply Theme to Folders.

And that's the not-so-Advanced menu.

The Window and Help menus

These two menus don't have much going on, or at least not much to do with iDVD itself. The **Minimize** (Command-M) command in the Window menu stashes your project window in the Dock. That way when you want to work on it again, you won't have to relaunch iDVD and wait for everything to load. Just click the Dock icon and your project will reappear on-screen.

Finally, the Help menu has only two entries: **iDVD Help** (Command-?) and **iDVD Tutorial.** The first launches Mac Help (if it's not already running) and displays the Help page for iDVD;

the second launches Mac Help (if it's not already running) and displays the first page of the iDVD tutorial (which we covered in Chapter 3).

The Buttons

The six buttons along the bottom of the iDVD window mostly duplicate functions on the menus, primarily for convenience (I guess). Left to right, they are Theme, Folder, Slideshow, Motion, Preview, and Burn.

As I mentioned earlier, buttons that do the same thing as menu items and keyboard shortcuts are included to placate Apple's powerful Department of Redundancy Department and its militant boss, Major Major Major.

The exception is the Preview button, which doesn't have a corresponding menu choice.

The Theme button

This button toggles the Theme panel open or closed. If it's closed, like this:

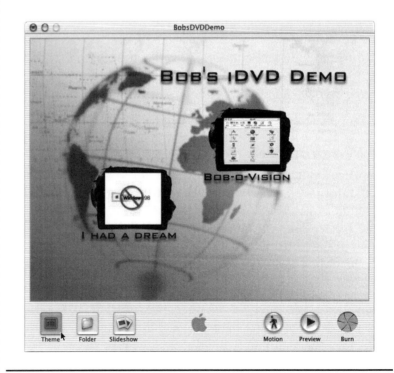

Clicking the Theme button will open the drawer, like this:

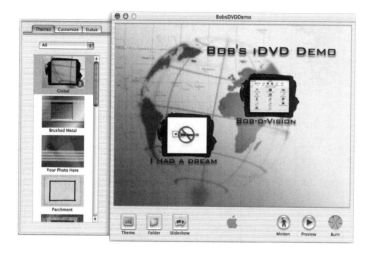

As you may recall, choosing Show/Hide Theme Panel from the Project menu and using the shortcut Command-Shift-B, as described earlier in the chapter, do the exact same thing.

We'll take a closer look at the Theme panel in the next section of this chapter.

The Folder button

The Folder button adds a new folder to the current screen. When you click it, like this...

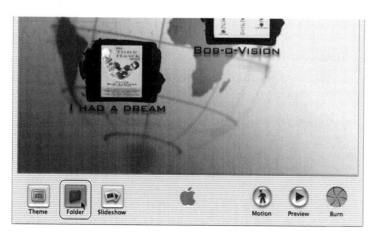

...a new button appears on the screen, like this:

If you want more than six items on your DVD, one of the items on the first screen absolutely and positively must be a folder. (Flip back to Figure 9.8 if you've forgotten why.)

Choosing Add Folder from the Project menu and using the shortcut Command-K, as described earlier in the chapter, do the exact same thing.

The Slideshow button

The Slideshow button adds a new slideshow to your project. When you click it, like this...

...a new slideshow icon appears on the screen, like this:

Choosing Add Slideshow from the Project menu and using the shortcut Command-L, as described earlier in the chapter, do the exact same thing.

The Motion button

The Motion button toggles your project's motion menus on or off.

Choosing Motion from the Project menu and using the shortcut Command-J, as described earlier in the chapter, do the exact same thing.

Regardless of which technique you use to turn them on or off, the Motion button emits a soft green glow when they're on, like this:

And, of course, it doesn't glow when they're off, like this:

Motion

The Preview button

The Preview button lets you test your DVD before you burn it. When you click the Preview button, you get a genuine simulated remote control that looks like this:

Use its arrow buttons (or the arrow keys on the keyboard) to select an on-screen button. A selected button will have a border and its title will change colors, as shown in **Figure 9.9.**

Figure 9.9 An unselected button (left) and the same button when selected (right); note the color of the title and the border around the button when it's selected.

Use the remote control's Enter button (or press the Enter key on the keyboard) to activate the button.

You can also click directly on an on-screen button to activate it.

Activating a button causes its movie or slideshow to play full-screen. When the movie or slideshow is finished, the DVD menu reappears.

To exit Preview mode, either click the Preview button again or click the Exit button on the remote control.

The Burn button

Finally, the Burn button burns the project onto a blank disc.

Choosing Burn DVD from the File menu or using the short-cut Command-P, as described earlier in the chapter, do the same thing.

If you have motion menus in your project and they're turned off, you'll receive a warning first...as you saw in the section about the File menu.

One minor difference between the button and the Burn DVD menu item or keyboard shortcut is that you must click the Burn button twice. The first time you click, the radioactive "ready to burn" icon will appear, like this:

The second click prompts you to insert a blank DVD if you haven't already, like this:

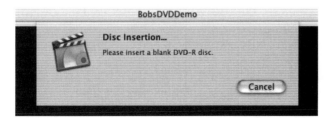

Once you've done so, go have a cup of coffee or something. Your finished DVD will pop out of your SuperDrive when it's done.

The length of time a burn takes depends on the amount of material on your DVD. If you have more than an hour of video, the burn may take more than an hour. If you have 5 minutes of video and a small slideshow, the burn will take less time.

The Theme Panel

The Theme panel, which you've now learned how to show and hide three different ways, lets you select and modify a theme, which can be applied to one or more of your menu screens.

But what, exactly, is a theme? In iDVD parlance, a theme is the visual look of the screen, including its background image and audio, the title's position, font, color, and size, and the buttons' position, font, color, and size.

You can pick a theme from the 14 that come with iDVD, or create your own theme using the techniques discussed in Chapter 6.

Now let's look at the items in each of the Theme panel's three tabs.

The Themes tab

To select one of the 14 themes in the Themes tab, just click it. As soon as you click a theme, it's applied to the current screen only.

To apply the theme to every screen, choose Apply Theme to Project from the Advanced menu; to apply the theme to folders only (and not to your main screen or other non-folder screens), choose Apply Theme to Folders from the Advanced menu.

Themes that include motion backgrounds sport a circle that resembles the Motion button, such as this one:

Wedding

Click the Motion button to see the motion in all its glory. (And click again when you get sick of it.)

Finally, there's a pop-up menu at the top of the Themes tab that looks like this:

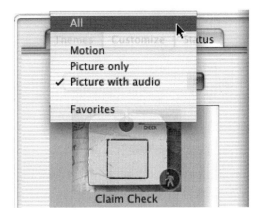

It lets you select which themes are displayed:

- **All** (14 themes to start with)
- **Motion** (10 themes)
- **Picture only** (four themes)
- **Picture with audio** (one theme)
- **Favorites** (however many you select, as described in the next section)

The Customize tab

The Customize tab, shown in **Figure 9.10,** is where you tweak your themes. You can choose the background image or movie and audio; the title position, font, color, and size; and the button position, font, color, and size.

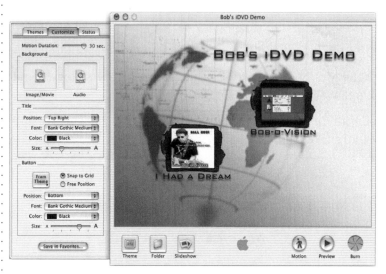

Figure 9.10 The Customize tab lets you modify almost all elements of your themes.

The **Motion Duration** slider at the top of the Customize tab determines how long movies play before repeating themselves. Slide it all the way to the right for the maximum length of 30 seconds; slide it all the way to the left to have no motion at all.

This duration is used for both background movies and all of the motion menu buttons on the current screen. There's no way to set a different duration for the background and buttons, nor is it possible to set one button to a 5-second duration and another to a 10-second duration.

The **Background** section controls what you see behind the buttons and folders on the screen, as well as what music (or other audio) you hear.

If you're using a background video and don't specify a particular audio file, the soundtrack of the background video will be heard instead.

The two rectangular items you see in the Background section are "wells," which are targets for dragging-and-dropping from the Finder, as shown in **Figure 9.11.**

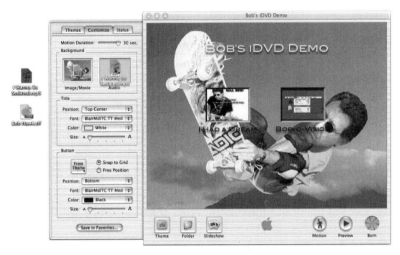

Figure 9.11 I'm dragging an MP3 file (the Ramones classic "I Wanna Be Sedated") into the Audio well.

For example, I first dragged the image file "Bob Hawk.tif" into the Image/Movie well. As you see, that image (of my head grafted onto Tony Hawk's body through the magic of Photoshop) is now the background screen.

Next, I dragged the MP3 audio file "I Wanna Be Sedated.mp3" into the Audio well.

The net result is that whatever picture and song you drag in are what you see and hear when the DVD loads.

You can also use the File menu commands Import > Audio, Import > Image, and Import > Background Video to specify the background audio, image, and movie.

The **Title** section lets you customize your title text (*Bob's iDVD Demo*, in the preceding figures) in several ways.

The first item is the **Position** pop-up menu, which offers five choices:

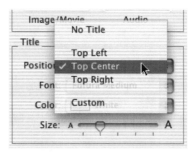

No Title, of course, means what it says—the screen will have no title text. The next three choices—Top Left, Top Center, and Top Right—put the title at the top of the screen, inside the TV safe area. The final choice, Custom, is the most flexible; it lets you drag the title anywhere.

"Anywhere" includes outside the TV safe area, so be careful.

The **Font** pop-up menu lets you choose a font for the title. The **Color** pop-up menu lets you choose a color for the title text. And the **Size** slider makes the title larger (slide it to the right) or smaller (slide it to the left).

The **Button** section lets you customize your on-screen buttons. The rectangular button at the top left is actually a pop-up menu. Press it (click and hold) and the button-shape menu appears, as shown in **Figure 9.12.**

The radio buttons to the right of the button-shape menu let you choose to have your buttons snap to an invisible grid (and thus not be "moveable"), or be freely positioned, which lets you drag them anywhere on the screen, as I've done in Figure 9.12.

The **Font** menu lets you choose a font for your button labels (Bank Gothic Light in Figure 9.12). The **Color** menu lets you choose a color for your button labels (Dark Brown in Figure 9.12). And the **Size** slider makes the button labels larger or smaller when you drag it left or right.

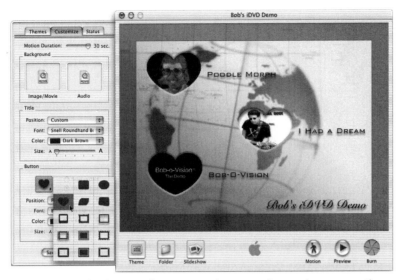

Figure 9.12 The button-shape menu lets you choose from more than a dozen shapes.

Finally, the **Save in Favorites** button allows you to save a custom theme, featuring all the things you customized in the Theme panel, as a "favorite." When you've tinkered and tweaked and are tickled with the result, click it. You'll be asked to give this favorite theme a name:

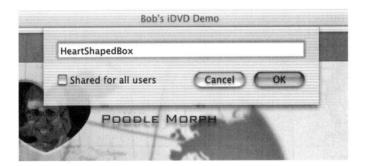

If you click the "Shared for all users" check box, this theme will be available to all users of this Macintosh; if you don't, only you will be able to use it in the future. Either way, when you want to use the theme again you'll find it in the Themes tab, under the Favorites menu or when you select All:

 If you decide you no longer want a Favorite you've created, just delete it from your hard disk. Shared favorites can be found in /Library/iDVD/Favorites; your personal favorites are in /Home/Library/iDVD/Favorites.

The Status tab

The Status tab provides feedback about background encoding of your movie files, plus a running tabulation of the total duration of the movies in your project. In **Figure 9.13,** you can see that the Celebration movie is already encoded, the Play Time movie is halfway done, and the Beach movie has yet to be encoded. The total duration of all three movies equals 1:58 (1 minute, 58 seconds).

Figure 9.13 The Status tab tells you what's been encoded and how much video is in your project.

The Pit You Throw Your Money Into

I told my publisher this chapter was required, kind of like a warning label—if the film-and-DVD-making bug bites you, I hope your pockets are deeper than mine. This is a heck of a hobby, but it can get real expensive real fast. I speak from experience. I find myself lusting for bigger, faster, better, and cheaper hardware and software to satisfy my near-insatiable need.

Of course, you can spend a small fortune on the toys for actually shooting your video—your cameras, lights, microphones, tripods, Steadicams, and all those other accoutrements of more professional shooting.

But you absolutely don't need to spend a lot of money on software to make good movies and videos for your DVDs. But you could, and it wouldn't be hard. Software for this particular slice of heaven comes at a cost.

Fortunately, you have everything you need to make a movie or burn a slick DVD already. You don't *need* any of what follows.

But you'll probably *want* at least some of it.

Figure A.1 There are entire Web stores like www.videoguys.com, devoted entirely to the latest and greatest gear you can buy for your camera or your Mac.

I know one guy who actually bought a little trolley-thing that runs on rails, to use for those smooth tracking shots you see in "big" films. And another guy who had to have his living room floor reinforced to hold all the video and audio gear. But I digress.

Since my specialty is the Macintosh, I'll spend the rest of the chapter showing you new and exciting ways to empty your pockets directly into your editing and DVD mastering studio (a.k.a. your Mac's hard drive). I've already covered hardware you can spend your dough on in several places in the book, but software has gotten short shrift.

This appendix is the antidote to that. Get out your MasterCard and get ready to spend some quality time spending quality money for quality software.

Budget-Priced Software

But before we get to the bank-busting stuff, here are a pair of consumer-priced software goodies that give you a whole new arsenal in the editing studio. And, as of this writing, both had free samples available!

Two companies I know of offer inexpensive packages of transitions and effects for iMovie at really reasonable prices. And both of them have at least a few you can download and sample for free, and use forever without obligation.

Virtix Special Effects

A little company called Virtix (www.virtix.com) offers three free special effects, with no time limits, watermarks, or other restrictions involved in using them.

The first is the *Flame* effect:

It adds the flames you see in the foreground, with full control over height and intensity.

Bad pun alert: This gives new meaning to the term "burn a disc."

Moving right along, the second one is the *Extreme Black and White* effect:

It converts the colors of your images into full-on black or white, with no shades of gray, for stark, high-contrast, abstract images.

Finally, there's an adjustable *Letterbox* effect for giving your movies that Hollywood look:

Virtix also sells more than 50 special effects and transitions in several different combinations and packages, none of which costs more than $40.

Here's a by-no-means complete list of Virtix's offerings: Blur Edges, Edge Detector, Emboss, Extreme Color, Funhouse, Heat, Laser, Lightning, Median, One Color, Pixel Fixer, Rain, Smoke, Sparkle, Sparkle By Color, Spins, Stained Glass, Topograph, Tunnel, Zoom, Burn Through, Clock Wipe, Crystal Fade, Dream, Flying Blocks, Fog, Materialize, Materialize Flicker, Page Peel, Pan, Shatter, Shrinking Tiles, Smoke, Sparkle, Sparkle Aperture, Swirl, Vertical Bars, Wipe, Normal Zoom-In & Zoom-Out, High Quality Zoom-In & Zoom-Out, Snap Zoom-In & Zoom-Out, Static Zoom, Spotlight, and Witness Protection.

Although you probably wouldn't use most of them every day, they can really make your movie stand out from the rest of the pack.

Slick Transitions & Effects and Slick's Spice Collection

These two sets of effects are aptly named—they are slicker (pun intended) than a Texas roadway after a spot of rain. Made by a little company run by an old buddy of mine, Bruce Gee (www.geethree.com), the Slick packages are the best value in iMovie-making today. In fact, he has a quote from me right on his Web site:

Bruce, like many of my old friends, is a former Apple employee.

We used to call him "Squee." Get it? Squee Gee. Squeegee.

Anyway, he worked on the PowerBook, Newton, and other cool stuff you've used or heard of.

GeeThree is his proof that there is life after Apple. So far, all of his products (the three I've tried—Slick Transitions and Effects 1 & 2, and his Stealth Serial Port), have been stellar—inexpensive, useful, and updated regularly. And, of course, Mac first and Mac only.

These simple but elegant add-ons can spice up your iMovies, but they're as easy to use as iMovie itself. And Bruce gives you nine of them, absolutely free.

The freebees include Heart Open and Heart Close:

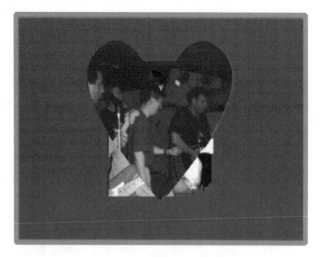

Burst:

And six more, including one I've still never found a way to work into anything I've edited. I do love the ultra-cool X-ray effect, maybe I can work it into some rock-video parody:

The Slick Sampler, a collection of nine fully functional plug-ins, is available as a free download from www.geethree.com.

But the inexpensive collections are also worth looking into. I've had them both for a long time and get lots of use out of them. They're worth every penny.

Volume 1 is called Slick Transitions & Effects. For $30 you get 50 new transitions and effects for iMovie 2. This collection of plug-ins gives you a boat-load of digital effects similar to those that used to be available only in expensive editing programs. The transitions include Page Peels and Curls, Barn Doors, Doors, Blinds, Rotate, Spin and Tumbles, Zoom, Heart, and Star. There are also more than a dozen special effects, which alter the appearance of your video footage. They include the following:

- Film Noise, for that film-noir aged look, complete with scratches, dust, and color fade
- Mosaic, to give your footage that pixelated look used by shows like *America's Most Disgustingly Vicious Criminals* to disguise the identity of the "perp"

- There's Diffusion, for that slightly out of focus, psychedelic-cum-Impressionistic effect:

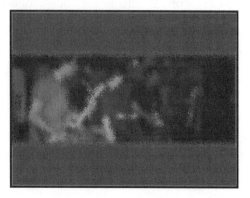

- I'm not sure I'll ever get to use Emboss, but its 3-D metallic look is pretty neat:

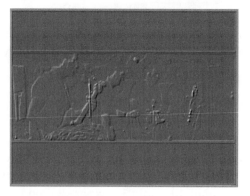

- And one I've gotten a lot of use out of already, though it's becoming somewhat the video cliché, Camcorder:

There's also a sequel, known as Slick Transitions & Effects Volume 2: Slick's Spice Collection. It has more than 50 additional transitions and effects suited for documentaries and independent films, as well as video projects for home or school.

But I'm running out of space, so you'll have to visit the GeeThree Web site (www.geethree.com) and visit the Gallery to see samples of the effects in each collection.

Both sell for $29.95, or get 10 bucks off when you buy them both. A CD-ROM is available for an additional $5 each.

I don't know the people at Virtix, but I've known Bruce forever and he's, as we say in the old country, a real *mensch*. You can do business with him with confidence. And do tell him I sent you. He probably won't cut you a better deal, but you never know. You're welcome to give it a try.

The Apple Pro Products

Well, that's about it for budget-priced options I'd recommend. But if you have the dough, Apple makes some of the coolest high-end video editing and DVD mastering programs on the market today—Final Cut Pro and DVD Studio Pro. Priced at $1,000 each, they're definitely not for the faint of heart or wallet. But if you find yourself "hitting the wall" with iMovie or iDVD, they're the first things I'd consider. Let's take a quick look at each.

Final Cut Pro

Final Cut Pro 3 (FCP) is Apple's professional-grade nonlinear video editing system. And when they say "pro," they mean it—Final Cut Pro has been used to edit major motion pictures, television shows and commercials, music videos, and more. It can edit almost every video format and resolution, from plain old DV like your camcorder spits out to film resolution good enough for 35 mm projection.

But what's remarkable is that you can perform almost the whole editing and post-production process in this one program. In addition to being a great editing application, FCP also excels at capturing video, managing massive numbers of files, adding motion effects, color correction, animated titles, and compositing unlimited layers.

It's more complicated than iMovie (duh), but it's not horribly hard to use, and the results can be spectacular. **Figure A.2** shows a typical FCP editing session in progress.

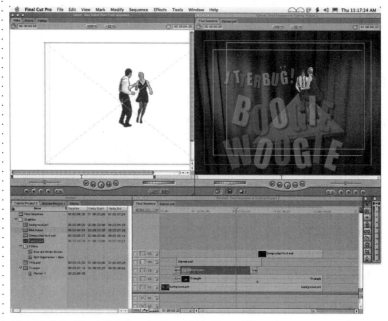

Figure A.2 Final Cut Pro is like an entire editing bay on a single monitor.

Or, as Apple likes to put it, "With G4 real-time effects, OfflineRT, and top-notch color correction capabilities, it's like getting $50,000 worth of editing tools for under $1,000."

But not much—FCP sells for $999.

The two breakthrough features in version 3 are OfflineRT, which packs five times more footage on your hard disk without any loss of quality, and G4 real-time effects, so you can see wipes, fades, and other transitions and effects without having to wait for them to render. The coolest thing is it all works on a Power-Book G4 Titanium, so you could, at least in theory, edit and post-produce your next masterpiece from almost anywhere in the universe.

As I said in the introduction, all those pages ago, I used to be in the advertising business, and edited a ton of video with the meter ticking away at $300 an hour. Today I can do better work, and do it faster and a whole lot cheaper, all without leaving the comfort of my office. That's just too cool.

DVD Studio Pro

DVD Studio Pro is Apple's professional DVD authoring tool. I'm not as familiar with it as I am with Final Cut Pro, which I use pretty regularly. But I haven't hit the wall yet with iDVD. I'm still satisfied with what it can do.

Someday, I'll probably want to do some things I can't do using iDVD, such as

- Interactive buttons and links
- Up to 99 video and/or audio tracks
- Up to 8 audio streams per track
- Chapter markers
- Multilanguage support, with up to 32 subtitle streams per track
- Dolby Digital AC-3 format audio
- Web links
- 16:9 format
- DVD-5 and DVD-9
- Output finished projects to DVD-R, DVD-RAM, or DLT. Unlike iDVD, DVD Studio Pro will happily burn to an external SuperDrive.

Figure A.3 shows DVD Studio Pro in all its glory.

When you rent or buy a big Hollywood movie on DVD, the kind with so-called bonus features, you can bet the disc was created with DVD Studio Pro or something similar but harder to use.

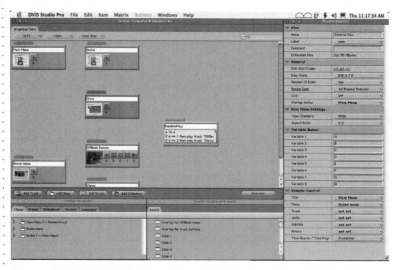

Figure A.3 DVD Studio Pro: It's not simple, but it's probably the easiest way.

While $999 might sound like a lot of money, that gets you more than just the DVD Studio Pro application. You also get:

- **QuickTime Pro.** Converts QuickTime files to MPEG 2 for DVD Studio Pro.
- **A.Pack.** Quickly batch-encodes audio into Dolby Digital.
- **Subtitle Editor.** Makes it easy to add them.
- **Peak DV.** A decent enough audio-editing program.
- **Corel Photo-Paint 10.** It's not Photoshop, but I actually like a lot of things about this program. It's included to allow you to build layered menus and other graphics for use in DVD Studio Pro.
- **FreePlay Music Library.** More than a gigabyte of music, absolutely free to use any way you like.

As I told you, I haven't spent much time with DVD Studio Pro.

OK. I admit it. It just came out and I only received my copy yesterday. So I haven't spent any time with it, save the few minutes necessary to install it and take its picture.

Lacking anything more of any substance to say about DVD Studio Pro, I'm going to move along now.

Other software you might consider

Gosh. That's a tough one. I'd have to recommend Adobe Photoshop, which can be used for masking, retouching, titles, animation, and more, and is the industry standard for serious graphics work. I use it every day and version 7, the first one made specifically to run under Mac OS X, is just great. In **Figure A.4** you see me preparing a screen shot for this book in Photoshop.

Figure A.4 This is it: Photoshop, the industry standard for working with graphics.

Photoshop sells for around $600. For a few dollars more (well, more like double that), you can get the whole Adobe Digital Video Collection, a suite of excellent programs that includes Photoshop, Premiere, After Effects, and Illustrator. If you're considering Final Cut Pro, this bundle is certainly a formidable and credible alternative. All four programs are best-of-breed and the package saves you around $1,000 compared to buying the individual applications.

You'll find all that Adobe software at www.adobe.com or any decent retailer of Mac goodies.

Finally, and even I admit this one's pretty geeky, there's the Cleaner family of compression products. If you're a pro, you'll need something like this to squeeze every last drop of performance and image quality out of your video files.

In **Figure A.5** I'm encoding a 2-minute movie.

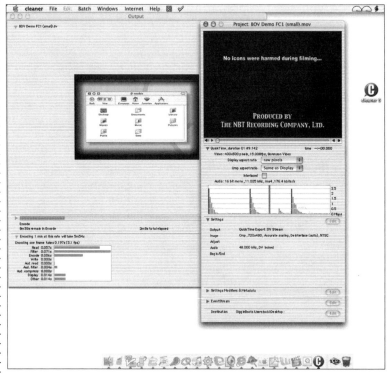

Figure A.5 Cleaner encodes faster and offers more control over the process, resulting in smaller, better-looking video files.

Find out more about Cleaner at www.discreet.com/products/cleaner.

Compression for Smart People (the MPEG Story)

In Chapter 3, I said, "We'll talk more about encoding in Appendix B." So here we go. What follows is a discussion of compression and encoding, with an emphasis on the MPEG-2 compression and encoding used to create DVDs.

What, Exactly, Is Compression?

Whether you realize it or not, your Mac probably uses compression nearly every day. Almost anything that comes with an Installer uses compression, and many file formats, such as GIF, JPEG, and PDF, have built-in compression and decompression. If you've ever seen StuffIt Expander doing its thing on your Mac, chances are it was decompressing a compressed file of some sort.

So what's this compression thing all about? Do you care? Do you need to care?

In the simplest terms, compression makes files smaller. Smaller files use less disk space and travel faster. As for whether you care, if all you want is to make some DVDs quickly and easily, the answer is a qualified, "no." Compression goes on "behind the scenes" or "under the hood." You don't see it but it's almost always there. And just as you don't need to know what's going on under the hood of your car to drive it, you don't need to know one iota about compression to make yourself a darned impressive little DVD.

But I believe that the more you know, the better your decisions can be. Since compression affects almost everything you do with iDVD (and with your Mac itself), you probably should know something about it (even though I just said you don't have to).

But first, we interrupt this chapter for an acronym break. As you know, where technology goes, acronyms follow, and DVD-making is no exception. So before we travel any further, here's a brief explanation of some common video and DVD-making word jumbles.

I won't waste trees defining them here. If definitions interest you, you can find better ones than I'll ever write and a whole lot more at Web sites like http://mpeg.telecomitalialab.com/ and http://bmrc.berkeley.edu/frame/research/mpeg/ mpeg2faq.html.

The Obligatory Acronyms

JPEG: Joint Photographic Experts Group

MPEG: Motion Picture Experts Group

TIFF: Tagged image file format

GIF: Graphics interchange format

CBR: Constant bit rate

VBR: Variable bit rate

AIFF: Audio interchange file format

fps: Frames per second

NTSC: National Television System Committee (U.S. TV standard)*

PAL: Phase alternating line (European TV standard)

VCD: Video compact disc

SVCD: Super video compact disc

DVD: Digital versatile disc (a.k.a. Digital video disc)

MP3: MPEG-1 layer 3 audio

* *Video professionals often joke that NTSC actually stands for "Never Twice (the) Same Colors," because the standard allows for a lot of variation.*

Enough MPEG to get by

Though iDVD makes things easy, there's more to making a DVD that will play in a consumer DVD player than meets the eye. For one thing, the video has to be encoded in the proper format. In the case of DVDs, that's a format called MPEG-2.

I'm going to hit the high points of MPEG-2; if you want the down-to-the-bone nitty-gritty, with all the mathematics and buzzwords included, check out http://mpeg.telecomitalialab.com/ and http://bmrc.berkeley.edu/frame/research/mpeg/mpeg2faq.html.

But merely being encoded in MPEG-2 is not enough. To play back properly, the bit rate (data transfer speed) has to be within a certain range, the frame size has to be just so, and various support files must be on the disc and in the proper directory (folder).

MPEG-2 isn't just for making $5 DVD-R discs, either. SVCD is another format that uses MPEG-2 compression. SVCD can record up to 80 minutes of video on inexpensive CD-R discs.

And that's enough about MPEG to get you by.

Compression types

Most compression algorithms (methods or recipes) are designed to work best on a particular type of data. Different schemes excel with different types of data—text, graphics, video, audio, or whatever.

Whatever the technique (algorithm), compression comes in two flavors: *lossless* and *lossy*.

You use lossless compression when you want to lose nothing in the compression and decompression process. It's the proper choice to reduce the size of files containing text (such as word processor or spreadsheet files), or any other file that needs to be *exactly* the same when decompressed.

StuffIt, ZIP, TAR, and some flavors of TIFF and GIF use lossless compression. **Figure B.1** shows the effect of compression on a 1 MB folder.

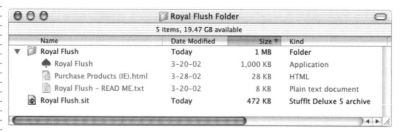

Name	Date Modified	Size ▼	Kind
▼ 📁 Royal Flush	Today	1 MB	Folder
🔺 Royal Flush	3-20-02	1,000 KB	Application
📄 Purchase Products (IE).html	3-28-02	28 KB	HTML
📄 Royal Flush - READ ME.txt	3-20-02	8 KB	Plain text document
📦 Royal Flush.sit	Today	472 KB	StuffIt Deluxe 5 archive

Figure B.1 StuffIt Deluxe's lossless compression shrinks the Royal Flush folder by more than 50 percent!

StuffIt turned a 1 MB folder (Royal Flush) into a 472 KB archive file (Royal Flush.sit).

There are 1,024 kilobytes (KB) in a megabyte (MB).

When decompressed, the 472 KB StuffIt Archive will yield a 1 MB folder identical to the original, without having lost a single bit or byte.

The other flavor is lossy compression. It's called that because some data is always thrown away forever when the file is compressed this way. In most cases, it's data that doesn't affect the way the file looks or sounds after decompression, or at least doesn't affect it too much. JPEG and MPEG are types of lossy compression.

Figure B.2 shows the effect of lossy compression on a low-resolution picture (a screen capture). The one on the left is compressed around 25 percent, and doesn't look much worse than the original. If you were displaying this graphic on a Web page, the compressed version would load faster.

Figure B.2 Compare the slightly compressed (bottom left) and highly compressed (bottom right) JPEG-encoded pictures to the uncompressed original (top).

Figure B.3 shows the result of JPEG compression on a high-resolution photo.

There are three sets of pictures in Figure B.3. Each set has six images: The original 5.1 MB high-resolution TIFF file, four JPEG-compressed copies, and the Finder window displaying their sizes. The set in the lower right is actual size, the middle set is magnified 300 percent, and the set in the upper left is magnified 600 percent.

The 25 percent setting applies the least compression, but produces a file one-fortieth the size that looks almost identical to the (bloated) original.

The 50 percent setting applies a bit more compression, and yields a file even smaller—a mere 88 KB. But as you can see in the magnified sets, you're beginning to get some image degradation.

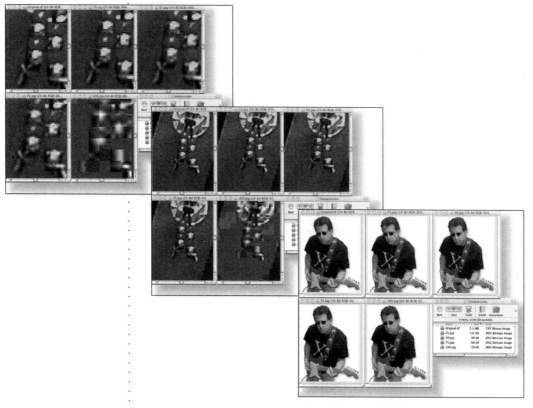

Figure B.3 The more compression, the lower the image quality.

You'd rarely use compression settings as high as 75 percent or 100 percent in real life, but you can see what happens to an image when you do—detail is lost and image quality suffers. Sure the files are even smaller, but now they're ugly.

Video compression works almost the same way—the more similar each frame is to the ones before and after it, the more compression you can apply without ill effects.

There are many other ways to reduce the size of a movie file besides compression. The two most obvious are reducing the frame size and the frame rate. The smaller the image, the less disk space required; the fewer images displayed per second, the less disk space required.

Beyond these rather brute-force techniques, though, you'll find a plethora of compression schemes for video involving the use of one *codec* (compressor-decompressor) or another.

The codecs used for video CDs and DVDs are different flavors of MPEG. Other codecs that QuickTime can use include DV Stream, Sorenson, Animation, and CinePak, to name just a few. The one that's most important to you at this time is DV Stream, since it's the format iMovie feeds to iDVD.

Why Some Pictures (and Movies) Compress Better Than Others

You'll soon find out that some files compress better than others. Some will continue to look great even after you've saved them with high compression settings. Others display visible "compression artifacts" even if you save them using low compression settings. Furthermore, some files shrink a lot and others shrink a little.

Why is this? The technical reasons could fill a book, and have—more than one, too. But the simple explanation is that the less complex an image is, the better it responds to compression.

I selected the picture in Figure B.3 not because I have a gigantic ego, but because it exaggerates the effect of compression. It has a relatively small color palette (I know it's black-and-white here, but trust me on this one) and large areas of the same or similar color (the white background, the black T-shirt, and the red guitar in particular), so it can withstand a lot of compression before you notice the image degradation.

One thing you'll notice about video compression is that it decompresses a lot faster than it compresses. It isn't unusual for compression to take five or more times as long as decompression. The main reason for this difference is that during compression the data has to be analyzed to determine which compression techniques need to be employed. During decompression, that analysis is unnecessary. See the discussion "Down to the Real Nitty-Gritty" below.

At the end of the day, it all comes down to this: the more compression, the worse the image quality. Compression is good, but there's such a thing as too much of a good thing. Don't overdo it.

I have two more compression tips for you before we move on.

1. Start with the best raw materials you can.

   Remember that compression removes detail that can never be put back. It's like toothpaste—once it's out of the tube it's nearly impossible to restore. So the better the image or footage is to begin with, the better it will look after compression.

   This is a variation on the well-known GIGO (garbage in, garbage out) theory.

2. Use a tripod whenever possible.

   Unnecessary camera movement is the enemy. The less you move the camera, the better compression will work (and look). If you can't use a tripod, stabilize the camera against something like a wall or tree to minimize accidental motion.

Many set-top DVD players choke on SVCD and its older brother VCD. In fact, even some DVD players that claim to support SVCD or VCD don't. Try it before you get too excited about squeezing 80 minutes of video onto 20 cents worth of disc.

Down to the Real Nitty-Gritty

The rest of this chapter is optional. You don't have to know the technical details that follow, but, as I said earlier, the more you know, the better your decisions are likely to be. If minute details are your thing, you'll love it. If they're not, I won't be insulted if you move along right about now.

Movies are usually filmed at a rate of 24 frames per second. NTSC displays (roughly) 30 frames per second. But each NTSC frame is divided into two "fields," each containing half the information for the frame. So it's essentially displaying 60 fields per second, with each field holding half the pixels for a frame. The only way that can happen is if each frame is compressed.

An MPEG-2 encoder creates a compressed movie file by analyzing each frame and deciding how to encode it. Much of the compression is identical to that in, for example, JPEG, eliminating irrelevant data. It also compares information from other frames to reduce the overall size of the file. Each frame can be encoded in one of three ways:

- An **intraframe** contains the complete image data for that frame. This method of encoding provides the least compression.

- A **predicted** frame contains just enough information to tell the DVD player how to display the frame based on the most recently displayed intraframe or predicted frame. This means that the frame contains only the data that relates to how the picture has changed from the previous frame.

- In a **bidirectional** frame, the player uses the information from the surrounding intraframe or predicted frames. It approximates the position and color of each pixel. (Techies call this *interpolation*.)

As I mentioned earlier in the chapter, the type of scene you're shooting has a large impact on the types of frames used and the amount of compression applied. The more action, the more intraframes will be needed; the more intraframes needed, the less the frame can be compressed.

On the other hand, a shot of a talking head against a still, single-colored backdrop will use a lot of predicted frames, which will result in greater space savings with minimal quality loss.

Your DVD player reverses this process as it pulls data off the disc and reconstructs the frames (decompresses) to display on your TV or monitor.

For even more information, one of my favorite Web sites is How Stuff Works (www.howstuffworks.com). In particular, check out the write-up of DVDs at www.howstuffworks.com/dvd.htm. It's a massive article:

If you want to know more, start here. Like all the stuff on How Stuff Works, it's chock-full of beautifully executed illustrations like this:

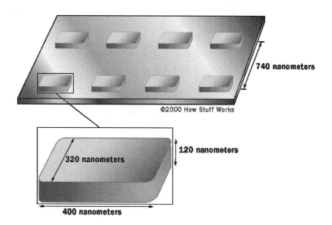

MPEG-1, a.k.a. VCD

Before there was MPEG-2, there was MPEG-1, which was the basis for the original VCD (video compact disc) format as well as the (in)famous MP3 format and associated revolution.

VCDs require MPEG-1 files that conform to the *white book* specifications—a series of rules describing frame size and bit rate as well as the *muxing* (short for *multiplexing*) of the video and audio streams.

Toast Titanium from Roxio (www.roxio.com) is the program I use to make VCDs.

VCD (NTSC) video has a 352 x 240 frame size, a frame rate of 29.97 fps, and audio sampled at 44.1 kHz stereo. The quality of VCD video is about that of VHS, assuming that you had clean data to start with and used good tools to do the encoding.

Remember what I said before about GIGO? It really matters when you try to make a VCD.

MPEG-2, DVDs, and SVCDs

SVCD quality can approach that of DVD. In fact, most people (including me) can't tell the difference. SVCD video has a 480 x 480 frame size, a frame rate of 29.97 fps, and 44.1 kHz audio.

OK, how do you create these VCDs and SVCDs? Well, the VCDs are easy, assuming you have Toast 5 Titanium. You just create your movie in iMovie, choose Export to QuickTime, and select the Toast VCD option from the Export dialog's pop-up menu.

SVCDs, on the other hand, are a royal pain in the bottom, since there isn't really a good (or at least good and inexpensive) MPEG-2 codec available for the Mac. Yet. You have to step up to iDVD's big sister, DVD Studio Pro (see Appendix A), or a full version of Cleaner with MPEG Charger (www.discreet.com/products/cleaner/) to produce MPEG-2 files. But that's not the end of it. Once you have MPEG-2 video, use the freeware GNU VCDToolsX to create Toast-ready image files, then produce your SVCDs using Toast's Multitrack CD-ROM XA format option.

> *Although much of the "how to" information is slanted to Windows users, www.vedhelp.com is an excellent source of information about VCDs, SVCDs, what DVD players they're compatible with, and just about anything else you want to learn on the subject.*

DVDs, of course, also use MPEG-2 compression. Most professionally produced DVDs use VBR (variable bit rate) encoding, where high-action scenes are encoded at a higher bit rate than relatively action-free scenes. iDVD uses CBR (constant bit rate) encoding, where all scenes are compressed at the same bit rate—it just uses a lower constant rate for 90-minute DVDs than it does for 60-minute DVDs.

> *Even the miniDV format used by your camcorder employs compression. This compression is called DV-25 and has a constant 5:1 compression ratio.*

If you want to use VBR like the pros and be able to get even longer movies on your DVD-R discs, you'll probably need to spend a lot more money (again, Appendix A has details).

Beyond MPEG-2 (MPEG-4/DivX;-))

But wait...there's more: There is a specification for MPEG-4 that's optimized for streaming video and is based in large part on Apple's QuickTime technology. Then there are MPEG-7 and a draft for MPEG-21. Don't ask me about the numbering, though, because I haven't found out what goes in the holes, either.

MPEG-4 is sometimes referred to (albeit incorrectly) as DivX;-).

Yes, the smiley is part of the name. And it has nothing to do with the abortive "pay per view" DVD alternative offered by Circuit City and others.

DivX;-) is an offshoot (some say bastardized) version of MPEG-4 that first saw widespread distribution in the Windows world as a Microsoft-specific variation of the MPEG-4 specification. There is no real standard for frame size or frame rate. I've seen DivX;-) files with resolutions of 720 x 360 (wider than widescreen) at 24 frames per second at the high end, and 200 x 150 at 15 frames per second at the low end. There doesn't even seem to be a standard for audio, although MP3 at 48 kHz is common.

Although there were ways to view some DivX;-) movies in OS 9, the OS X tools are better and are updated at a rapid pace. A quick check of VersionTracker for "DivX" will provide all the software you need.

Were I to mention specific programs, they would almost certainly be out of date before the printed copies of this book hit the bookstores, much less your hands.

So go. Download DivX;-) software and give it a try. You just might find it more fun than making DVDs!

And that's all we have time for. I could go on and on, but my editor keeps bugging me about actually finishing this thing so we can all go home. And actually, I've covered the best stuff already. So adios!

P.S. Drop me a line at littleidvdbook@boblevitus.com and let me know how your burning is going.

Index

S

W

Z